Dedicated to Kudzai, Ruby and Rosie,
my beautiful grandchildren. You inspire
hope in a future filled with love,
acceptance and fun.

May you ever keep smiling.

Published in the United Kingdom
in 2017 by MPire Books of Crewe
Copyright © Rob Wykes

Cover design by Glen Battams.

# IT'S NOT ABOUT THE FURNITURE

ROB WYKES

# CONTENTS

# ENDORSEMENTS

'Inasmuch as you did this unto the least of these my brethren, you did it to me' (St. Matthew, chapter 25 verse 40).

This beautiful book demonstrates the meaning of this verse. One way or another, St. Paul's has been at the service of the people of Crewe for nearly 150 years. Long may if flourish.

The Rt. Rev. Dr. Peter Forster, Bishop of Chester

*It's Not About the Furniture* drew me in at once to the world of St. Paul's Centre, the charity operation in Crewe where Rob Wykes and his merry band of colleagues tackle some of society's most entrenched problems -poverty, hunger, and homelessness - with faith and second-hand furniture. Wykes writes with intimacy and a large dash of humour about the challenges and triumphs St. Paul's has faced over the years, weaving together a story that is by turns amusing and inspiring. Above all, this book is a testament to the mysterious workings of faith, to how God aids those in greatest need, restoring hope and dignity to lives that once seemed lost. I was moved tremendously by this story, and heartily recommend it to anyone interested in the ins and outs of Christian charity work in the twenty-first century.

Macy Halford, Author of *My Utmost: A Devotional Memoir.*

# INTRODUCTION

This book is an invitation to join me on a journey, watching people. We all do it, whether in the street or sat at the railway station. It can be a fascinating experience, and we all learn something every time we gaze into someone's life.

In September 2016, I sat with my wife, Cheryl, at an awards evening in the grand surroundings of Crewe Hall. There was no expectation of recognition. In fact, I assumed my name was added to the nominees to make up the numbers. Genuine surprise and humility washed over me as the announcer read out my name, linked to the words 'Pride of Crewe.'

The central focus of the award recognised my twenty years leading the work at St. Paul's Centre. However, reflecting on that wonderful honour, I find myself challenged to tell you about the many individuals of whom we should all be proud. Some were damaged by drugs, some were beaten by depression or faced the daily grind of broken dreams. Each one offered a story of hope as they became part of the community at St. Paul's Centre, a remarkable expression of Christianity.

*It's Not About The Furniture* is an account, but not a clinical diary, of the people and events that have shaped the charity. The following pages offer a collection of my memories, an interpretation as I saw things unfold. A preacher and story teller at heart, I have been careful to bring honesty to the recollections I now invite you to enjoy. If, having read the last page, you wish that you had met one of the incredible characters described within the book, or you retain a smile at the many humorous incidents, then your reading will have served you well.

Finally, dear reader, in purchasing this book you are contributing to the ongoing work of the charity. In reading it, you will discover what change your continued support can bring.

Rob Wykes

## THE JANUARY SALES

The snaking queue finally started to move. I was incognito; a large winter coat and a flat cap hopefully sufficient to render me anonymous to most of the regulars that mixed with over one hundred huddled bodies before me. They rubbed hands, shuffled awkwardly and blew quick blasts of warm breath into the chilly January morning air. There were easily ten different languages spoken, all excited despite the cold that enveloped them.

My watch said 9.30am. It was time, and the heavy door creaked open. Like those ahead of me, I swung one weary foot after the other, slowed by the icy conditions but keen to enter the relative warmth of the vast church building that towered above the line of worshipers below. And yet none of those gathered had come to pray at St. Paul's in Crewe. This was a wholly different congregation; practical rather than spiritual. And for once, I wanted to stand on the other side of the fence and witness what others discovered when they entered our humble charity.

The rows of heavy furniture arranged either side of the main entrance was a clue to what awaited the visitors. Pricing labels were placed strategically to entice and inform. Conversations about potential purchases took place along the line as the morning sale was officially declared open.

There was a real buzz now, and the cold was soon forgotten as everyone received a warm welcome. There was also a smile and personal greeting from several enthusiastic staff who were eager to please. They were cheerful and genuinely keen to help, a credit to us all. For now, I remained at a safe distance. The masses had come to buy tables, chairs, fridges and bric-a-brac. I didn't want my cover to be blown.

"Hello," offered one of the ladies by the door, determined to engage with me as she already had with dozens of others. "Morning," I muttered in reply, head bowed, wondering if I could possibly slip through unnoticed. It sounds strange, but I didn't want the staff to feel that I was snooping. I wasn't, just curious to see what others uncovered as they explored the hidden treasures within.

As I edged past, turning away as though embarrassed by my actions, a feeling of immense pride flooded my veins. What a wonderful way to treat people, affording each and every one the time and courtesy all human beings should be given every day.

By now the masses were funnelling through the great door with a sense of expectation, all out for a bargain. They had purpose; I stuck out like a sore thumb as I looked on in awe, bewildered and beguiled in equal measures as more figures streamed past me. The ministers of old had become modern-day sales staff – watching, directing, advising and transacting. For a few moments, it was a blur as the people flocked inside the once magnificent Victorian church… this was now St. Paul's Centre.

The visitors could be divided into very distinct groups. Canny traders sought gems amongst the bric-a-brac; perhaps vases that concealed Royal Doulton pedigree, or fancy goods that had value only the trained eye could see? Others perused the paperbacks ever hopeful that they might uncover a classic edition, perhaps with an inscription that would add yet more worth to the fading pages.

Homemakers came for sofas, chairs and tables, a dogged determination to line their nest perhaps masking the desperation of their financial circumstances. I prayed briefly that they would find what they needed, and at a price they could afford. A young family tested a settee almost to destruction, bouncing and jumping, stretching the springs beyond anything demanded by the original manufacturer. The kids had fun while the parents considered the price. Others craved white goods - fridges, washers, dryers and freezers, all tested and ready to be delivered.

Then the bike workshop caught my eye. It was now the engine room of the centre, akin to a mechanics' centre of excellence that would have enhanced any railway workshop of old. Tools graced every shelf, carefully stowed, labelled and ready for greasy action. There were rows of refurbished cycles, pedal power keen to be unleashed on the roads. Racks of parts were carefully ordered and priced way below what the high-street cycle retailers would charge. Wow, it all looked so professional. The trademark Crewe bike stood out, with its straight handlebars and reduced gears, suitable for a relatively flat town and the occasional up-and-over railway bridge. A middle-aged gentleman sized one up, transport that would take him to work and keep him fit. Another surge of satisfaction as I considered what we achieved each week, helping those in need, assisting others who just needed a leg up, and making lives richer for those with little material wealth.

My journey through the mayhem of the early morning sale took me down the church nave where, to the left, I looked to the old bell tower. It was relatively peaceful now, no chimes to be heard as the hardware and intricate mechanism had long since been removed. Instead, the rumble of bodies, dragged wardrobes and open/closed cupboard doors echoed around the vast space behind me.

Then, with the altar a few metres in front of me, shifting respectfully to the left, I picked up the scent of perfume, or maybe oil. It was the old vestry, now about beauty, therapy and massage, a safe-haven for women, somewhere to make them feel whole. Another part of St.Paul's reaching out to those in need once again, now helping to heal physical and mental health scars, addressing the anguish of enduring cancer treatment or other life-threatening conditions. Whatever the issue, the goal was to make those ladies feel beautiful again. The door was closed, locked even. But I knew exactly what was offered for those needing privacy and a little much-needed TLC.

I turned back again and walked through the arch, with the words 'Holy, Holy, Holy' embedded skilfully into the wooden screen above. Despite many years of internal changes, the rood screen remained intact, richly carved, separating the nave from the chancel. Harsh shafts of winter light flooded through the intricate stained glass panels and poured into the raised area that was once the altar. There, priests had once broken bread and served wine in remembrance of the one depicted in the window above. There was no communion today, but a design still flickered in my mind to one day utilise the area and maximise its potential. Offering coffees and cakes from this point would be a different kind of service, and another way to provide people a welcome.

Immediately to the right of the altar the organ loft still bore pipes that had delivered hymns of worship for over a century. Music was no longer an option, at least not from any keyboard that would have originally been played by the skilled organist. The chatter of voices today was a wholly different sound. Those voices were louder than the hushed congregations that sat absorbing sermons, but nothing compared to the mighty notes that would have resounded around the church when hymns were the communal sing-along of choice.

Then, to the right, through heavy plastic strip curtains, there was a factory feel. It was time to drop my disguise. This area was out of bounds to the public, and there was an industrial vibe. There was the food bank, St. Paul's Pantry, housed in the old organ chamber, with the loft still rising high up above me. There wasn't a crisply struck note to be heard; just the clank of tins as volunteers arranged the food donation products into categories ready for distribution. We were feeding the soul on the left-hand side of the altar, and the body to the right. It could have been mid-summer, not January, as my body glowed with pride as I watched the good work around me.

When I continued, and walked through the lady chapel, I finally met the man, St. Paul the Apostle. He looked down from on high as another stained-glass window projected his colourful image on the parquet floor below. But there was no time to ponder. "Shift over, Rob," was the gruff but polite request. I nodded an apology and duly stepped aside.

A wardrobe swept past me, cunningly balanced on a delivery trolley. There was action and life everywhere. I needed to get out of the way. There was work to be done.

Once upon a time my journey around the Victorian church would have ended there. But not now. I skipped up the stairs, not an original feature, a metal addition that allowed me to travel into space. After the charity's operations and reach expanded, we had created a new mezzanine floor to add value and further storage options. It did all that and more, but also afforded much-needed quiet so that I could briefly collect my thoughts.

There was bed alley, row upon row of mattresses stored ready to be delivered to young families in need of one of life's essentials. It was a tempting site, the perfect spot to grab some privacy and a nap after exhausting meetings. It was a fleeting thought, as another of the centre's volunteers breezed down the manufactured corridor en route to distribute another mattress. Getting them down to the waiting vans outside was back breaking work, and always hand-balled by volunteers. I needed to move on again.

Next up was what looked, to the untrained eye, like a jumbled stockroom. Closer inspection revealed a clever system of racking that housed bedding packs, pushchairs, cutlery, pillows, utensils, and various starter-pack combinations for young or needy homemakers. Everything had its place. These items were not for sale. They would go out to those who needed them and could not afford to pay. Providing those vital life accessories was at the heart of what St. Paul's Centre has always set out to achieve, but it goes much deeper than that. The countless hours preparing those packs of essentials had provided work and fulfilment to many people involved at the centre. Those benefits were largely unquantifiable, but ultimately priceless. Giving people a sense of worth was an ongoing journey that would be delivered via many vehicles. This was just one.

Now I reached a junction. A series of offices appeared through various doorways, with staff engaged in daily administration tasks. In some of those surrounding rooms, also created since the charity expanded, there was industry, learning and laughter. Before I could move on, I was immediately greeted by a group of enthusiastic and beaming young adults. They were busy upcycling mirrors and stencilling old pieces of wood from otherwise unusable furniture. Nothing should go to waste. They were happy in their work. Their output would add value on many levels.

In one of the centre's main offices, at the west end of the building, another glorious stained glass window came into view. It was a vision that always engaged me. Christ dominated the ornate glass pieces, with children gathered around receiving his blessing. The words 'Suffer the little children come unto me' put everything into context, but there was more. A passage towards the foot of the window, spread across several panels, recognised the services of the church's second vicar. Arthur Henry Webb, brother of well-known railway engineer Francis William Webb, served St. Paul's Church between 1887 and 1910.

The final phase of my personal tour took me down the stairs that had been added to connect the mezzanine with the reception area. For a few moments, I briefly returned to the hustle and bustle of the sale, cutting across the entry porch as people were still making their way in, while others were leaving with goods acquired.

Another out-of-bounds area appeared, but even on sale day it was up-and-running to another group. In fact, it was a hive of activity. This was a wholly different aspect of what St. Paul's Centre now offered. The space before me was a conference room, part of the old vestry hall that had served as a school room for many years. Now it had multiple functions, today alive with the buzz of computers. Those machines sat on trolleys, very portable, with people tapping away, a new way of learning amid ancient surroundings.

My intention was not to disrupt, especially with a young adult education class in full swing, so I took yet another set of stairs to another mezzanine floor. The enterprise zone connected St. Paul's Centre with the commercial world, and with other not-for-profit groups. There, housed in compact units framed by carefully crafted wooden arches that were part of the original church structure, were individual working spaces. Heads bobbed and looked at my familiar face. There was a busyness, a sense of purpose. This was a hot-desk haven for those who needed a digital space amidst olde-worlde surroundings.

The loft was perfect. No two businesses were alike - social projects, freelancers and council officers who dropped in to use the facilities. Modest rents were paid to utilise St. Paul's Centre connectivity; some used the bays for no charge as their contributions were made in many other ways that helped to paint a much larger picture for the charity.

As I walked back down the stairs and into the hullabaloo of the Friday morning chaos, it hit me: "It's not about the furniture," I said out loud, attracting bemused looks from the latest arrivals to the sale. "It's so much more than that…"

## A FIVE THOUSAND-MILE JOURNEY

The narrative from the opening chapter is a snapshot of what St. Paul's has become. It's taken many years of perseverance, heartache, setbacks too numerous to mention, joyous celebrations, and slow but steady progress.

My brief tour that chilly morning, through the charity's labyrinth of rooms, workshops and abundant storage areas, represents the collective achievements of many dedicated people. Over time they have pooled vast experience, countless resources and unbridled determination to create a humble not-for-profit organisation that has always maintained lofty ambitions. The centre's development is ongoing, and it has already formed a significant part of my life.

The journey that ultimately led me to the sturdy door of a deconsecrated church is winding, but worthy of note for the direction taken and decisions made.

So…my backpack stowed, I turned and hugged my sister, Pauline, then Mark, my closest friend and greatest supporter, before boarding the bus bound for London, from my boyhood home of Coventry. It was Saturday, April 14, 1984. Two weeks earlier, I had bought a ticket that would change my life for ever.

I was settling into a window seat near the back when a small, silver-haired lady asked if the seat beside me was taken. "No, it's not," I told her. She introduced herself as Mary, and explained that the purpose of her trip was to visit her sister in Ealing, West London. Excitement was written all over her, and housed in her face shone a childlikeness which twinkled in her eyes.

The coach pulled out of the bus station and glided up the slip road giving a clear view of the cathedral spire rising from the centre of the city. We both enjoyed the view and savoured the moment, but Mary was curious about where I was going. "Athens to start with, and then… well, I'm not sure. You see, I want to discover what lies beyond what I know."

It's a strange thing for a young person to speak of 'discovering' something beyond, because often what they mean is to escape, run away and avoid what is the present. Mary looked at me with knowing, wise eyes and began to tell me about her life.

In 1940, aged just 18, Mary worked in the Alvis factory making armoured tanks for the war effort. It was hard graft and not very lady-like spending your days with oil and grease covering your clothes and hands. She understood the need for this because two of her brothers were fighting in Egypt. At some point during most working days a siren sounded, and everyone ran for cover. It was tough work, always darkened by the sinister clouds above.

Mary remembered November 14, 1940, the night of the Moonlight Sonata air raid, as though it were yesterday. People from the four corners of the world visit Coventry to see the shell of a burned out cathedral. Visitors marvel at the new cathedral and artwork depicting reconciliation. The city is defined by that one night. Winning football trophies, producing famous pop singers or educating a future Prime Minister will never overshadow the scar on this historical landmark.

Mary smiled as she recounted the visit of King George VI after that November night's German attack. "Robert," she said, "you cannot imagine 500 aeroplanes dropping bombs; we all knew someone who had died."

Seeping through her words was the sense of despair and confusion that she had experienced the night of the raid. How could a people subjected to such horror survive - no, more than survive, rebuild a city?

Thoughts flowed through my mind, questions about what good could war ever bring, and who benefitted from any large-scale destruction and killing? As I pondered these complex and unanswerable questions, plus many other thoughts about how God - this person who was beginning to enter my life - could allow it all to happen, Mary said: "But in the middle of this I found love."

Well, blow me away; this silver-haired, 62-year-old woman sitting next to me was getting younger by the second. She went on, describing a faint but decipherable cry for help that came from behind a wall that night when she walked through the ruins. "Help!" she emphasised. It was a man's voice - but whom and what she would find if she investigated had troubled her at the time.

Fearing the worst, with images of mangled bodies filling her head, Mary slowly inched her way through the rubble. The destruction was such that it was hard to work out which bit of the house she was standing in. There were hissing sounds from broken pipes, and crackling, burning timber was masked by dense smoke. She moved a window frame with its glass pane remarkably intact, and there, lying motionless, was a leg. The boot lace was in several pieces; the trouser leg ripped. Was it just a leg? About three inches above the knee, a large sheet of thin wood lay still.

Then it came again, that low but distinct cry for help! Clearing the wood, Mary saw a dusty-faced young man smiling back at her. He lifted his head, and said: "Is this heaven?"

Three children and forty years of marriage later, our bus pulled into Victoria Station, London. From that moment, I realised that the great adventure for me would be to travel into the lives of other people. Mary had the most amazing story to tell, and yet she had not ventured beyond Coventry most of her life.

More than thirty years have passed since that bus trip which led me to journey through Greece, Turkey, Iran, Pakistan and India, ultimately returning via Russia. That is a tale for another occasion.

The point is that we all have a story to tell. Occasionally, we can share our story. Whether on a long bus journey, or over a garden fence, we all have opportunities to exchange experiences. A silver-haired lady shared just enough of her life story to leave me, like a drug dependent man, wanting more. Mary's tale was sufficient to instil in me an unquenchable thirst, of wanting to show interest, to watch and work with people for the rest of my life.

So here is the story of a charity, thought by many to be simply a furniture reuse centre, seen through the prism of the people who with passion and creativity envisioned something not in existence, but something that was possible to achieve.

Along the way some were built up and made alive; others were broken by the toil, disheartened by the human conflict that happens when we rub shoulders together. It is a story of people, not a building; yet the building at times seems everything. At times the theme is hurt and pain, loss and dysfunction. But mostly it is the story of human triumph - of people who saw what could be, not what was.

Some unknown writer crafted a great sentence that I took to heart the moment I heard it. They wrote that faith is the assurance of things hoped for, and the certainty of things yet to be discovered. My early days of exploring faith led me to this conundrum; I have it, but I don't. Explaining my faith or story, any faith or story, usually ends with similar... that you grasp it, or you don't.

Sometimes we need a sign. In 1936, a gentleman called Alistair Cooke attended the one hundredth anniversary of the founding of Harvard College. He expected it to be less than memorable, although President Roosevelt was to speak. Amidst the lengthy proceedings, as Roosevelt made his way to the podium, a student standing near to Cooke remarked that the president seemed to have trouble walking. Such was the collective denial of the president's polio, few people ever realised this.

Sixty years later, Cooke reflected on the student's remark. For him, it was an artless remark, a taproot if you will, into a visual memory of that day.

For me there was a similar visual memory. During my first week working at St. Paul's Centre I discovered that pens went missing. They were not stolen, just stored in the pockets of a young man in the office. If you wanted a pen you just asked him. He was a short man with an evergreen smile; Rich was his name. Our director at the time was a man much bigger than Rich, and very strong. I walked in one day to the sound of laughter, along with some low shouting. John, the director, was holding Rich upside down by his ankles and shaking him. Pens were falling from every pocket. Everyone in the office had the look of fear that they might be next!

As Alistair Cooke would say, right there before my eyes was the one visual memory of that day that remains indelible. That, for me, was the moment. I knew then that I was in a unique place that could never be replicated.

Years earlier, at bible college, we were shown how man had landed on the moon, swam the most hostile seas, and explored the deepest forests. Those amazing feats had been achieved. In fact, exploration in general is done and dusted but for the journeys into the souls of human beings. That quest is never ending.

The opening pages of this book hopefully emphasised the huge variety of services that the centre now offers to so many people. It certainly is much more than a furniture store. Quite how it became so much more is the story I hope to tell, from the man who had a vision to create a church, to those who took on the challenge to run a charity, and to many more who have stood by my side and experienced so much, St. Paul's is the vehicle, enabling me and others to engage with individuals each day.

Over subsequent chapters I will attempt to detail some of the wonderful people who have lit up my life and allowed me to enjoy their most amazing journeys. Their stories ARE what St. Paul's Centre is all about, a journey into the souls of men. I can only hope that I do them justice.

## COLLABORATION & COMMITMENT

The way we leave this world speaks beyond the way we enter. That we are born within interesting circumstances, or come from a line of nobility, is in the end of passing interest. Reaction to our leaving does, however, speak much of us.

The funeral procession for John Ashe, during which much of Crewe stood still, spoke of a man the town had taken to heart. This small community came out in force to show respect for someone who had served them well. The local paper reported that Ashe was a generous public benefactor, a warm friend to the poor, and a tremendous comfort to many who suffered.

Whilst in the throes of death John Ashe attended the funeral of an old friend, Mr. Beech, which took place during a violent downpour of rain. That said much about the man, putting personal comfort to one side so that he could support another. It probably didn't do him any physical good, such was his weakened condition by then, but that was of little consequence to a man with a heart of gold.

His heart, however, was cause for concern. Medically, we have an explanation of what caused the body of Ashe to shut down; an inflammation of the bowels and liver. Yet there is another, more painful reality to his demise, for Ashe had a broken heart.

The death of his beloved wife early in 1878 had all but finished the man. A week before his friend's funeral, he took on another Sunday service, but he was so overcome that he was unable to continue to the end. Everything about this man cried exhaustion and brokenness. It seems he gave everything he had to the work and community he loved. It is highly possible that this was only sustainable whilst his courageous and supportive wife Susan was close by his side.

That same Sunday, after he left the pulpit a defeated man, he made a brief recovery before a relapse in the night, and early on the Monday morning he died. With daughter and son-in-law at his side, and wife gone ahead, he had no real desire to recover. After saying he was ready to go and that his work was done, he left.

St. Paul's Church, Crewe, is a bit of a landmark, standing at a crossroads close to the town centre. On any given day, the latest of the town's mayors might visit for a tour, one of many that take place throughout the year. Most folk are greeted at the door with smiles and hearty handshakes, then ushered into the director's office for tea and stories. They walk around the centre - more smiling faces - and soak up the atmosphere. For a moment, they feel transported into a small and very different world within a world. "Every town needs one of these," the mayors usually say.

There is only one Crewe – a unique town with a unique railway heritage. There's only one St. Paul's Church with its unique founder,

John Ashe. And there's only one St. Paul's Centre. All of them were born from the dreams and visions of a handful of men whose stories and histories overlap.

At the time of writing, there have been 185 years of Crewe, 147 years of St. Paul's Church, and 30 years of St. Paul's Centre. Through those years, the world has changed beyond all recognition; yet for the poor and marginalised the struggle is the same as it has always been. The solution is also the same. Time and love are what make a difference. And there are men and women today who, like Ashe, have caught a glimpse of the heart of God that has not only changed the direction of their own lives, it has ultimately impacted the lives of others. They are people who continue to believe – like Jesus himself – that no-one is beyond hope. Were it not for the belief in people, and willingness of Ashe to collaborate with the railway companies in 1865, St. Paul's would not have come into being.

Arguably, the only certainty we can hold onto in this life is that everything changes. Buildings and people, landscapes and communities come and go. But something of our stories – the people we are and the things we do – remain in the fabric of our surroundings. Whether we recognise it or not, the legacy of who we are and what we've done is invisibly passed from one generation to the next. Hopefully it will be one that enthuses generations yet unborn to do similar, leaving legacies of their own to inspire those who follow behind them. In this sense, buildings are more than simple bricks and mortar. They represent the dreams, joys, sorrows and challenges of the lives that have been lived out in them.

It is easy for us amid stressful and busy lives to become disconnected both from our history and from each other. We may even question the relevance of a community's history to anything going on in our hectic lives today. But leafing through photos of how things used to look, and peering into the faces of yesterday's people, we may feel the sudden tug of an invisible thread which joins our lives to those who have gone before us. They lived in the same streets, had the same basic needs. They were different, but also, somehow, familiar.

Like it or not, our stories, like our footsteps, somehow overlap. We are mostly unconscious of how profoundly our lives have been shaped by those who've gone before us and we certainly doubt the power of our own lives to shape what is ahead.

What started out as a small rural platform back in 1837, the Crewe junction continues to be one of the most important rail intersections in the country. It later became one of the most historic railway stations in the world. By the 1890s, a thousand trains would pass through Crewe in twenty-four hours. Plans are progressing to bring the most ambitious railway development in modern times, a high-speed line named HS2, through Crewe around 2027. It seems wherever we live, or at whatever point in history we are, the tide is rising or falling. Ashe arrived in Crewe as the tide rose.

Ashe could see the room and need for a new church and committed himself to seeing it happen. He was a calculative risk taker who learned to seize opportunities and had once worked tirelessly to make something of himself. He made his fortune as a mill owner in Stockport turning out cotton. In fact, he had worked hard from a young age, made careful investments on the stock market, and became a wealthy man. Long forgotten and with little known of him, Ashe was a remarkable man. Breaking with the norm and considered late in life for such change, aged just 44, he left a prosperous life and joined the church.

Boom in the railway industry was taking place and Ashe was best placed to move when opportunity presented itself. His background in business and manufacturing would serve him as well, if not better than his theology degree. Given permission by the Bishop of Chester to buy land for a new church, Ashe set about raising the capital. He was a visionary, and before a spade was pushed into the earth, Ashe saw clearly what St. Paul's would look like. He was a man on a mission with the spirit of a pioneer burning within him.

Walking around Crewe it is plain to see that the railway companies were behind much of what remains of the fabric of the town today. They funded the building and upkeep of many churches; it was railway money that paid for Christ Church in the town centre – now a partial ruin. Ashe could see, feel and smell the growth all around him. The brutal clang of metal was everywhere as he travelled around, and sometimes those travels were to visit hard-pressed rail workers damaged by the heaviness of the industry. Ashe experienced first-hand that the advent of the railway was changing the face of the nation. This was a time when there was a desire to push back the boundaries, of innovation, self-belief and national pride. This small landmass, which still thought of itself in terms of a global empire, was producing men of great fortune and a nation of excitement, but from what Ashe saw the steam era was not romantic; it was a harsh pressure on the daily lives of his parishioners.

Capability notwithstanding, for reasons he alone knew, Ashe chose not to keep a journal and there are no remaining personal letters or effects to shed light on what may have made the man tick. Like so many we know of who left a story worth telling, we can only look at his activities and achievements and speculate about his thinking and feelings, his motivations and the driving passions of his life. Clearly Ashe was a remarkable man.

Typical of the day, the railway company minutes were wordy and full of detail. From these accounts, we discover Ashe to be a man of passion and commitment. Frequent reference is made to his request for help to build St. Paul's. That Ashe was a man of faith is not in doubt, but underlining his life's work seemed to be a drive to create a platform for others to build upon. Many men and women with the skills and academic capacity of Ashe would choose to leave a book, a poem or memoirs, but he left a building. It is the story of his life, a story to be found in the faces of those whose lives have been transformed through contact with St. Paul's.

Commonly, we hear of those who make use of their fortunes through their blessing of others. Indeed, the charity's work is in part made possible through Ashe's legacy. Today some of the beneficiaries are entrepreneurs as he was. However, Ashe was more than a cheque writer. He was happily married with a grown-up son and daughter. They had shared several lovely homes together, and could afford to travel. But for Ashe, and his wife, there had to be more to life than pleasure and comfort. They chose instead to come and live among the rows of blackened brick terraces which stretched endlessly into the distance, the length and breadth of Crewe. Not exactly a quiet country residence for this family!

In some ways, Crewe must have had the same sense of urgent industry which they had known before in Stockport. Smoke belched relentlessly from hundreds of chimneys as mothers clipped the ears of their children, scrubbed steps and peeled potatoes. Dirty hands and faces were the norm. Diseases spread like wildfire because of the poor and crowded housing conditions. The unrelenting beat of the Works' hammer sent vibrations through the walls of every home and the ground beneath their feet as more than 20,000 men and women beavered away producing everything for the rail industry.

Choosing, as Ashe and his wife did, to live alongside the people they came to serve tells us so much about their hearts and humility. In so many ways their lives reflected echoes of Christ and his teaching. They had encountered something powerful enough to move them. Faith, it would seem, overshadowed comfort. We can only guess that they understood the injustice that life is not only sometimes hard for some people, but that for some it is always hard. They wanted to live that life so that they could fully understand what others encountered.

In those dark industrialised days with smoke hanging low over the town from the coal fires, an image of hell to some, Ashe found hope and a way of seeking light. The Ashe family became part of the ordinary working people of the town. Sharing hardship for them included spending time in sub-standard housing helping sick people often towards death.

Powerfully influenced by his Bible and 19th century theology, Ashe held out a hope that the men and women living in rows of terraced houses would encounter God as he had. That they mattered to God and their lives were of infinite value would have been words readily to hand as he paid his visits. The account of his activity in the town reads like a one-man crusade to heal the sick, educate the poor and turn the tables of injustice experienced by the rail workers. He wanted to see them reach their true potential. He longed for every child to be able to read and write, believing this had the power to reveal whole new worlds of opportunity and imagination. He wanted his God to lift their heads, to give them the confidence to pursue their dreams. Ashe's dream was to impart hope, dignity, confidence and opportunity. He clearly felt the weight of this responsibility to make a difference.

Passionate about the need to change the spiritual landscape of Crewe, and it would seem with no other reason to build St. Paul's Church than needing a vehicle for the cause, Ashe started a mission. Initially, he was curate at St Michael's Coppenhall. From this vantage point he reached out to where St. Paul's now stands. Following his actions, we meet Ashe the strategist and vicar. Gaining wide support from the churches around and the Bishop of Chester, Ashe began a weekly mission to 'convert souls' and create a congregation in the newly designated parish of St. Paul's. This was run in tandem with a series of engagements with railway businesses. He met in London with senior LNWR management, basing his request for support for a church building on it being needed for their workers. Ashe was tenacious. In some ways, he appears uncompromising.

Ashe had a vision of St. Paul's Church styled along the lines of a medieval parish church, fashionable at the time, with seating for 1,000 people. We can only imagine that he did not think small once he got going. As things transpired, the church only seated 680 when complete and had several changes to the original drawings, a story we all recognise from every building project ever undertaken. But this was a man with contacts, and his little black book was full of industrialists, entrepreneurs, socialites and philanthropists. As well as contributing from his own personal income, Ashe had influential friends.

The bit between his teeth, he saw the project effectively completed in two years. A man called J. B. Stansby, a railway company architect, took charge of the project. The sandstone used to build the church came from the cuttings into Liverpool Lime Street station. So, St. Paul's is literally built from the very rock dug out of the earth to make way for something else to be built.

This is a foreshadowing of what would happen again in the future, for since the mid-1980s, St. Paul's has been a centre for recycling and reuse in the area and this is exactly how the fabric of the building came about. By his own efforts, Ashe managed to collect the total cost for the build. Money came in from all over the country. In fact, he generated so much mail that the local post office was unable to cope with it. He regularly took boxes containing several thousand circulars to the general post office in Manchester. It took enormous energy and determination to see the job through. It was, at the very least, a visible demonstration to the railway workers of the extent of Ashe's commitment to them. He was a man of commitment with what at times seemed to be an inexhaustible reservoir of energy.

There is no sign that he withdrew that level of commitment until his death some thirteen years later. Were Ashe here today he would certainly acknowledge the part those he collaborated with played, in what was a monumental feat. On site, the high winds proved too much for the scaffold, stopping the work before it started. Daily pressure for more money and maintaining good relations with the number crunchers occupied much of Ashe's time.

To some the whole project was a distraction from the real work of building a railway; to others a delay in the preaching of the gospel. After all, Ashe was called to the ministry, not project management! Those in the church with the ability to stand back objectively admired and appreciated what Ashe was creating.

Ashe became buried in the detail to such an extent that he raised the money for light fittings and applied for free gas from the railway company's gasworks to be used for lighting the church. Not one to hold back, he turned to the railway for help in keeping the church warm, but was declined. During these days, there were moments of pure joy such as the opening of a letter with money. That would facilitate the signing of another legal agreement, ensuring the purchase of more vital resources or a much-needed permission.

Darkness also visited on days, as the railway company reminded him they were there for profit not religion. Ashe knew that earthly speaking, the task was impossible without them, yet his faith and trust in God held the tension to the end.

It's sad to see so many churches today reduced to piles of brick, mountains of rubble representing the prayers, the giving, the dreams and energy of generations of families committed to making a difference by making Jesus known. To Ashe the church he was instrumental in building, forming part of the Crewe skyline, was a representation of heaven itself.

The main body of St. Paul's is an amazing feat of engineering – the first church in the country not to be supported by aisles. Surely, only a railway architect and engineers could have pulled off a self-supporting roof space with no aisles or columns to obscure the view! This was for Ashe bound to the idea of removing barriers, and clearing a path forward. His vision was more expansive than the church building. That holds true for St. Paul's Centre of today.

William Jacobson, Bishop of Chester, consecrated St. Paul's Church on July 27, 1869. Impressed by its size, he joked: "Is it a church or a railway station?" But in the heart of Ashe the building represented a space for local people to meet with God. It made a statement. It said: "Look at me! Don't walk by on the other side. Come in."

Ashe was clearly either a man who was blind to problems but had eyes that were wide open to every possibility and opportunity, or else he was a man of unshakeable and outrageous faith – or maybe both. Perhaps the Bishop was nearer to the truth than he realised. For here was a place you could hitch a lift and begin a journey. The same spirit pervades St. Paul's Centre today.

Ashe was not a one-trick pony either. Passionate about education and its power to transform, he raised money and opened new schools, ran evening classes and organised training. And in the years following the church's completion, John Ashe was doing what he did best and, chasing money yet again, he stirred the vision to establish further schools in Crewe. He bought the land for St. Paul's schools, now on Adelaide Street, for £300. On top of that he raised a further £1,300 both from his own pocket and donations from churchgoers, which led the other Crewe clergy to give a further £200.

He worked hard to secure railway support because he was determined to run the schools as independent church schools, free from the influence of secular government school boards. The railway donated £1,500 and supplied company bricks at cost price. The schools opened in 1875 – divided into boys, girls and infants - and could accommodate up to 700 children. The buildings are still used today for children with special needs.

Surely, Ashe must have been a man with exceptional powers of persuasion, in that he could cajole seemingly endless funding from the pockets of such fearsomely powerful men. Possibly his business background combined with his new life as a vicar gave him a peculiarly assertive stance when it came to social justice. His experience as an employer and entrepreneur certainly made Ashe a force to be reckoned with once the spirit of God had taken hold of him.

There can be little doubt that this man was the driving force behind the building of St. Paul's. Even less doubt that he was, humanly speaking, driven by altruism. He cared deeply for the people that he believed God had called him to serve.

In becoming acquainted with him through the extracts that I have read, a comment of Paul the Apostle comes to mind. Ashe in much the same way as Paul had enjoyed an interesting life before faith in Christ. Therefore, we must accept something more powerful than personal ambition was driving them on.

In writing to the chaotic folk in Corinth, Paul uses the phrase 'the love of Christ constrains me.' Paul knew it was not experience, grit or clarity of vision that kept him at the coalface when the rock seemed too hard to move. It was for him, Ashe and every leader forging the way ahead, that the love of Christ is generating the energy to keep going. Ashe first and foremost felt called, not as a rich Victorian paying off his sins, but as a deeply blessed man moving out in personal faith.

## THE BIRTH OF A CHARITY

For a brief while following Bible College training, I joined the Railway Mission as a Chaplain. My primary role was to share my Christian faith with railwaymen and women. This led to hours of tea drinking and conversation. Such an experience was very fruitful. During those days, I discovered much about my own motivations. Through encounters with the pain and disappointments carried by those I sought to help, my own faith was challenged.

Faith, it would seem, is better shaped and strengthened through the crashing waves of fragile mortality, not the smoothness of warm sand and still seas. There were multiple encounters with people bearing complex needs, the likes of which I felt inadequate to respond to. Lines from the Bible and lofty unexplored ill-thought theology offered little practical solution to the widow facing a lonely life and mounting bills. Spending time with one man, poor, alone and struggling to raise young children left me angry with God. Daydreams of being financially rich and throwing money at problems often flooded my mind. Real experience, the source of gathered wisdom, however, tells us money is very rarely the answer. But it can help.

There were often funerals to conduct, sick people to visit and railway bosses' arms to twist for resources. Ah yes, did I not mention, I began the work as Chaplain to the North West with my hand full of begged tickets covering travel from Crewe to Manchester. No office, phone or budget. My first task was to convince a sceptic of faith that he should fund my travel. This exercise taught me the meaning of being as wise as a serpent and as gentle as a dove. Within three weeks I had a rail pass to travel at any time on any train in the United Kingdom. I learned that when God is in something, something will happen. It seemed to me that as I pointed others to the idea that God existed and was knowable, my own faith was tested. Forgive my impertinence, if that is what it is, but the more I spoke of God, the less I felt qualified to talk. To have faith is to believe in a realm and a person so radically different to ours that any encounter must be miraculous.

Life as a chaplain was not simple, and it was often challenging. Time spent in the presence of people helped me to see how desperately broken humanity can become. Yet on the other side of this coin of brokenness lies an image of resilience.

One day, I walked into a trackside work-hut to discover half a dozen men reading pornography, although there were few words on the page to read! The atmosphere was filled with hard indifferent male sexism. I was uncomfortable and they seized the opportunity to increase my discomfort. Stunned and scrambling in my mind for the right words to say, my silence left space for the hounds of sarcasm and taunt. I found myself gasping for purer air. Words were thrown around the hut and I was on my back foot until the eyes of a mature man met mine and we exchanged a knowing nod. "How's your Annie doing at college?" he asked of one of the ringleaders. The question rested on his ears - and as quick as the words came to me, I unleashed them. "The girl you're looking at is someone's Annie too." All eyes looked down – cups were quickly emptied as was the work hut.

Such encounters taught me to trust the words of Jesus recorded by Dr. Luke: "But make up your mind not to worry beforehand how you will defend yourselves. For I will give you words and wisdom that none of your adversaries will be able to resist or contradict." On that day in the hut, it sure did feel that the right words came at the right time. Tense moments were the ground on which I learned not to enforce morality without invitation or inspiration.

Over the next three years I would come to know the pain that people experience, pain that no number of apologetics or sermonising would abate. This was about establishing who I was and what my essential calling was. It didn't happen overnight, and there were times of searching - a screening of my soul. From this training ground I slowly moved towards St. Paul's Centre.

The literal journey began with a domestic crisis. One morning our electric cooker died. With income to the house so low that we qualified for some state benefits, buying a new cooker was not an option. Some use it as a joke but to us it was a living reality, to hear the one about the church treasurer's prayer: "We'll keep the minister poor, Lord, if you keep him humble." I was that stereotype. Our only option was to buy second-hand.

We had heard about a project based in a redundant church building in the centre of town, which we found easily enough. Confidently, people worked and moved around obstacles. There was furniture everywhere, and most eye-catchingly, a huge canoe suspended in the altar area. That was one of my first memories of St. Paul's Centre.

That the charity was up-and-running was a miracle. Less than four years earlier, the town planners had proposed a road widening scheme that began a debate that could have ended in the levelling of the church. Directly opposite St. Paul's sat a beautiful public house called the Chetwode Arms. It was believed to have been the town's original staging coach inn. The dilemma was whether to bulldoze the pub or St. Paul's. After a lengthy consultation period, where a vocal campaign was launched to save the pub, the local council voted to retain the church and demolish the Chetwode Arms. There was uproar because at the time the church's congregation had dwindled to a handful of parishioners. For some, the great tragedy came about a year later when the church commissioners deconsecrated St. Paul's.

So, the very existence of St. Paul's had once been under threat, and yet it had been given a new lease of life. Years later, I often ask people what they would make of a canoe suspended three metres above the altar area of a church. They look at me as though I have gone mad. To be fair, it did look odd – eccentric is probably a better description. And that's the first thing I discovered about St. Paul's Centre: there is a peculiarity, a sort of abnormality about it.

Long after the canoe had sailed from this altar area, with its organ pipes and a huge stained glass window, from which Jesus stares down from the cross, a woman standing in this space said: "It feels okay not to have faith here." I knew what she meant. St. Paul's Centre has a feel of acceptance – a sense that it allows you to be who you are.

Another time, a woman tapped me on the shoulder. "I used to sing in the choir here," she told me. "What you have done is disgraceful." I was taken aback, but immediately a man to my right who was looking at a piece of furniture, joined the conversation. "I think it's wonderful, a great use of the building. I was married on that spot," he said, pointing to the altar, "and if I had my way I would burn the place down!" He'd obviously had an acrimonious marriage. What it highlighted was the opposing forces that on one hand drove people to retain the ecclesiastical look, while others accepted that only practical uses could keep what is left of the church building alive.

On my first visit, when the need was a new cooker, a young man called Richard, showing us around, introduced John McCallum, a man with a presence. John was the energy and inspiration of the project. He wore one of those warm disarming smiles and I had an instant sense of connection. "Don't believe a word he tells you," John said, shaking my hand and nodding in Richard's direction.

John, the driving force and founding mind of what we now know as St. Paul's Centre, was a fidgety character – much like a boy always wanting to do the next thing. Along with a group of local Christians who met at the YMCA each Sunday following evening service, John galvanised a desire to reach out to the town's less fortunate. This was a young and dynamic group with more ideas than one organisation could accommodate.

So, how did St. Paul's evolve as the charity we know today? Well, with three million unemployed back in the mid-1980s - Margaret Thatcher is half way through her reign, and John, working for the Council for Voluntary Services, became frustrated. By 1986, John was irritated by the difficulties he found in both expressing his faith and doing good for people in need. Over time and through friendships, but with limited success, John encouraged the Gresty Road Church to get involved in community work. Greater support emerged from the newly opened YMCA who were looking outward towards the community.

Following a morning service in 1987, John remembers he and his wife, Denise, sharing a meal with Eamon and Christine Bundred, and Graham and Kerry Christopher. This is where the idea of Crewe Christian Concern found its first voice. As the assistant manager at the

Crewe YMCA, Graham found an overlap with John in their work at Crewe Council for Voluntary Service. Eamon was a theological student and had just moved with the Elim Bible College to its new premises at Regents Park, Nantwich. These three couples gelled in their thinking and were spurred on by a collective sense of frustration with what they saw as a lack of outreach to the marginalised by Crewe's churches.

John told me that many other people helped during the life of the project. It would be wrong to say that others didn't have a role in the organisation's creation. That said, I can faithfully say that the six of them were the first organised group who set up a sort of steering committee to progress the idea of the centre.

These three couples had key skill sets to get the ball rolling. John had community and environment written all over him. He was passionate about building a community and solving social problems. Graham had a concern for order and process. Eamon was an evangelistic and spirited man, the kind of guy who not only dared to have a go at things but he motivated others to move on the ideas they had. John said: "Eamon's ability to motivate the rest of us to do things, things we probably wouldn't have dared to do, drove us forward. Eamon offered a core vision for a long time. I personally think that without Eamon it wouldn't have got anywhere."

In those early months of the project the group met together to worship and engage with the residents at the YMCA. Their confidence growing, they decided to explore finding a building in Crewe town centre. Having a base for reaching out to people in the town seemed to be the right thing to do. At the heart of their thinking lay a sense that the space must accommodate people who felt uncomfortable in a traditional church setting. Reflecting, John said: "Our target was people that were socially isolated; many with problems such as substance abuse."

In the late 1980s, the national trends of growing unemployment and homelessness were starting to bite in Crewe. Traditional employment by the railways, Rolls-Royce and the sewing factories was still very influential and had been a shelter against governmental policics before the massive reduction in jobs that occurred in the following years. Crewe was a very traditional working-class town relying heavily on the extended family. You lived and died in Crewe and comparatively few people moved away, perhaps only to Nantwich or Sandbach if you aspired, or had delusions of grandeur! At knocking off time, the road alongside St. Paul's Centre was impassable due to the sea of workers on push bikes from the railway works and Rolls-Royce. Many young people were turfed out of home by their parents and had to live with other relatives or else obtain state funded accommodation, which was plentiful at the time. Crewe was in every way a working-class town with an obvious lack of middle classes.

Out of this declining backdrop emerged an expression of faith which became Christian Concern. John said: "We thought we might be the people to do something about it and enable local marginalised folk to find a living, something life-changing, find faith in Christ, as well as better their everyday lives through training, etc."

Passing by one day, Eamon saw and wondered at the sight of St. Paul's Church, empty and in the final stages of the redundancy process. Eamon dared to dream, sparking a chain of events that led to a 30-year and counting expression of practical Christianity.

There can be no doubt, whether you have faith or none, something about the timing and availability of St. Paul's Church speaks of a greater influence than human cleverness. St. Paul's had lost its parish status long before this, and the priest in charge had a declining congregation and a dilapidated building to deal with. For him, the emergence of a fired-up group wanting to do something with St. Paul's must have been heaven sent. I had already met Colin, the last Vicar of St. Paul's Church, during my work as a railway chaplain. He was a man who looked beyond the obvious, entertained the impossible and worked to remove obstacles.

John readily admits the organic nature and pace of the building transfer and project set-up meant that they didn't really know what they were getting into. "We were naïve and just rolled with the events," he would later admit. He believed that they made it happen. This was not the success of a well-thought-out plan, but an experience of pragmatic faith and the convergence of circumstances. Again, I would suggest a greater power was at work. Had they known the personal cost to setting the whole thing up, they might have withdrawn. However, support, volunteers and funds came in. It would be impossible to name even the key supporters there were so many.

As the CEO of the charity for the past twenty years, but with no involvement in the first ten years, it amazes me how many local people tell me that they helped to set up Christian Concern. From John's description of the early days – and the energy that surrounded it - hundreds of folk were significant in the charity's birth. History and this book must pay tribute to those three intrepid and courageous couples - people who put personal lives aside for a while, people who chased a dream, created a reality and built a bridge over which countless thousands continue to travel.

As I write these words, and most certainly as you read them, this charity is receiving income from space in St. Paul's let out to other organisations. We are enjoying a legacy income, if you will, from the decision those early pioneers took to buy the St. Paul's building. Owning the structure and deriving an income from it has been an enduring gift, and a recognition of their sacrifice.

In those early months and years, the community at St. Paul's was about people, not property, but a way to move from a chaotic idea to a legal structure had to be found. Eamon and Christine had become involved with the Teamwork Trust, a loose collective of charismatic fellowships across the United Kingdom. Local Crewe churches seemed lukewarm to the plans for St. Paul's – and their fear or lack of vision impacted John's attempts to involve them.

So, Teamwork Trust became more than an option; indeed, it was the only vehicle to move forward. They provided a charitable registration under which to shelter. In my view this was both a blessing and a curse – it was the start of a life of confusion for the project, and that confusion of identity rumbles on. Like a man unable to make up his mind as to what name to go by, the charity was born Crewe Christian Concern, merging with Teamwork Trust, to become known as 3Cs Teamwork. Over time, this became abbreviated to the 3Cs, only to return to Christian Concern, and is now rebranded St. Paul's Centre. I will explain the confusion later.

As 3Cs Teamwork they held a public meeting at the YMCA to formally launch their intentions. Graham was appointed the first project chairman, and John wrote a vision document to drum up support. Following a series of negotiations and complex ecclesiastical gymnastics, the diocese of Chester sold St. Paul's for £20,000. The local newspaper reported this to be the equivalent of an 8'x6' beach hut on Bournemouth sands. However, far from being a bargain, St. Paul's was in a state of disrepair, needing much work. The Church of England had sold a pup. Leaky roof, dry rot, poor defences and condemned electrics meant one thing – it was a money pit.

With help and prayer, John approached the Tudor Trust which resulted in a £40,000 grant. This investment contributed to securing the livelihoods of the (what is now) current seventeen paid staff and all the previous people who enjoyed financial, practical and emotional support over the years. The initial Tudor Trust grant remains the single largest grant the charity has received.

A million mini events took place to establish the work of the charity from this point forward, but one defining moment sparked the central and enduring core activity of the charity. On February 26, 1990, a seaside town in North Wales was flooded. Towyn hit the national news, and in the following days, what was the 3Cs charity responded. "It was our moment of glory - the making of our future credibility," was how John described the event. A key figure also stepped forward, acting as a catalyst for change. Strong, eccentric and full of character, Gwyneth Dunwoody, Member of Parliament for Crewe & Nantwich, had a one-off surgery near to the church. She came to St. Paul's and asked John if he could help by passing on donated furniture to the flood victims.

Towyn, like the entire North Wales coast, was both a popular holiday destination for Crewe folk and a place of retirement to the many older people originally from the area. A simple appeal in the local paper drew in enough furniture to fill the church and leave its hall bursting at the seams. The Wellcome Foundation, based at Crewe Hall, organised an articulated lorry to ship the goods. Such was the response that Towyn said: "Thanks, but we don't need any more!"

Donations, however, were still coming through the door. John appealed through the local press to ask if donors would mind if the surplus was given to local folk in need – and nobody objected.

Unintended as it was, this event became the birth of 3Cs' reason for operating a furniture scheme. For John and others, this diverted them from what they had originally imagined the charity would be about.

Prior to this event the charity was a nice idea but not really delivering much apart from an alcohol-free bar at events, and some general support for local groups. An entity, yes, but you might say it only truly began to exist with a focus after this point. "We began to believe we could reach people for Christ by ministering to their practical needs through furniture, and at the same time enabling others to gain employment and training as a by-product. The fact that it was also pretty environmentally beneficial was the icing on the cake for me," John would later say.

No one at that point in time imagined that thirty years later the charity would continue to help more than 1,000 families each year with furniture, food and refurbished white goods - including cookers!

For my family, in receiving a cooker from the charity, we joined the growing number of beneficiaries. Unsolicited, I received an invitation to be a Trustee. Such an opportunity had never presented itself to me. The world of boardrooms and strategies was alien to me, and the first meeting I attended was quite fiery. There were tensions. As a species, we have a strange capacity to hurt each other. We become entrenched in positions and are passionate about our rightness in them. A brief read of the letters of Paul the Apostle reveals how much Christians still retain this capacity to hurt and become embedded in being right.

Pam, the chair of Trustees, called and arranged to meet up for a chat. It transpired that John, the director, wondered if I might have a more active role in the charity. During the following weeks I was appointed Director of Pastoral Care, a strange and concocted title. Casting my mind back it was clearly an ill-thought-out title bearing no relevance to what I was invited in to do.

In the short time that I worked with John, I never knew him to be motivated by personal gain or desirous of personal glory. I learned from John that there is a cost to Christian ministry, and there are few who truly pay that cost to the soul. John McCallum, in much the same way as John Ashe before him, had given beyond his reserve tanks. He was fun and interesting to work with, and yet firm and directive whenever he needed to be. He was passionate about the organisation and embodied in every way the image, so over-used and misrepresented in management books, of a man trying to spin too many plates. John was known by everyone, and the first to be called when in need of help.

I firmly believe that little if nothing significant would have happened had he not forged forward breaking with the perceived finest management styles known. Was he a team player? No. Was he a skilful and strategic leader? No. Did he love, protect and champion his team? Absolutely! Did he have a vision and plan of where to go next? In his head, yes - and there with absolute clarity.

There is a great story in the Bible about Moses becoming tired from holding his hands in the air. A couple of his mates put a rock under him and stood either side to help him. If we learn anything from working together it must be that we need mates to keep us going. My reading of the circumstances, which lead to John inviting or engineering my joining the charity, is simply that John needed a mate to come alongside and take some of the strain.

As the nation watched in stunned silence the return of Princess Diana's body, after that fateful crash in Paris, I began to work at St. Paul's Centre. It was the first day of September, 1997, a Monday morning, and the clock chimed 9.00am precisely. Spiritually and emotionally confusing, the day was outside my comfort zone and I was thankful for its end at 5.30pm. Taking a pen and writing in my diary, the phrase 'God always gives us light in the darkness whilst we desire to do his will' entered my head and landed on the page. These must be words written by a wise saint other than me! I knew then and I have known every day since, that I am truly out of my depth, or as Matthew so aptly puts it, poor in spirit. In my own words, I am desperate for help. Without any hesitation, I regretted the decision to take the role.

Less than a year went by and John left the charity. Without wanting to overplay our significance, I liken what happened in the incident on Mount Nebo, in Deuteronomy 34, to how things appeared to me. Having led the nation through the trauma of the desert, a defining part of Jewish history, Moses had to let go. His path did not lie ahead. He lived and breathed the journey, carried the faithful and the unfaithful, those who opposed him and betrayed him. Moses, the great leader, standing on Mount Nebo looking at the land below, is an image that shakes me. We can almost join him emotionally, as he, in one breath draws in the air of the Jericho valley, eyes soaking up the images of trees and water and rolling hills – and in the next breath turns away. Moses may well have spotted where Joshua would soon lead the nation across the famous Jordan River, leading to 'the promised land.' But his journey is over and he faces a new horizon.

## NEW VISION, NEW PURPOSE, OLD STORY

In the weeks leading up to John leaving, I had been working towards the development of a business strategy for St. Paul's Centre. I had no idea what I was doing. I had no reason to at this point, as nothing in my life had given rise for such things. If you want a bath, you turn on a tap – you don't write a plan. This was my approach to everything. Decide what you're doing, and do it along the lines of least resistance. But now I was discovering complex and formularised ways to set, work towards and analyse goals. Everything had to be measured, reviewed and noted; acronyms were flooding in. SMART was the favourite of the day (Specific, Measurable, Attainable, Relevant and Timely). I was not unfamiliar with the term 'smart' but it nearly always had the postscript 'arse' when used by my school master.

Another, more sickly term was TEAM (Together Everyone Achieves More). Whilst I could appreciate the value of these things, it struck me that most of it was so blindingly obvious it took more energy to explain these ideas than to do what needed doing.

Later in our journey at St. Paul's Centre we created the John Ashe Hall, in which small enterprises could work. One of these small businesses is called Know & Do. Intrigued I asked what they did. "We cut out the middle bit," said Bernard, one of the directors. "The middle bit?" I asked. He went on to explain that many organisations are unclear about what they want to do, so they become bogged down in the detail, spending too much time over-analysing and exploring. His model was simply to know what you want to do, and to do it by cutting out the energy-sapping middle work.

I had no idea where the charity was up to in terms of finances or vision. With John being tired, and most of the project's direction being in his head, it was hard to see a way forward. It all felt a little surreal.

Can you think back to a moment when someone made a statement that at the time seemed normal, or just a little interesting but weightless? Well, one afternoon around three o'clock, John said to me: "I'm going home and I don't know if I'll be back." I innocently replied: "It's too late to come back today; I'll see you in the morning." John immediately turned, and said: "No, I mean I don't know if I will be back."

John didn't return on either that day or indeed on any other day. The Chair of Trustees contacted me a few days later to call a meeting of the board. John had resigned. A tiredness had hung-over him, the weight of carrying the project for years.

I realised then that we should greatly admire and honour those who spend their energy and life in service and sacrifice for others. It has always troubled me that the project did not have the funds or framework to give John a sabbatical. Without doubt his tiredness was from service, and I believe his rest should have been with the blessing of the board.

Jesus used an interesting phrase by way of instruction - go the extra mile. My sense is that the charity could have walked with John in his moment of tiredness towards refreshment. So, in some ways it felt like abandonment or divorce. You see, bakers were not innumerate when they placed thirteen buns on the tray and called them a dozen. The Baker's Dozen was an attempt to ensure no one was short-changed.

Since watching John walk away from the charity, I have attempted, if not always accomplished, to give people time. St. Paul's Centre is open Monday to Friday, and as much as possible we insist everyone has a weekend free. We close at 5.00pm to ensure people get home. Nobody in twenty years has been dismissed on medical grounds. Working with broken people can break you, and so we have worked hard to mitigate the possibility of short-changing others.

All eyes were on Pam as she spoke about John not coming back: "From today, Rob will be in sole charge. He is our appointed Director," she told everyone. From a standing start, I was asked by the Trustees to assess the position of the charity. Things were not good and the immense pressure John had been under had transferred to my shoulders. With energy and passion John had defied all the odds against him and built an organisation with assets and potential. Unfortunately, problems had developed. The charity sector, in my experience, is generally promised more than ever materialises. Some years begin looking full of growth and development, but they can end with redundancies and hardship.

Exploration of the charity's position revealed a flaw in John's character, a flaw I share and one I hope my successors will carry. We want to rescue people. We are what psychoanalytic therapists call 'the rescuer' type. The theory plays out in a drama triangle in which we over reach to rescue others and end up falling. On occasion, we forget how much we too need rescuing, and expend our resources so much that we are no use to anyone. When Moses sat on that rock we mentioned in the previous chapter, I believe it took a lot for him to accept help. He was the one holding things together, leading from the front, willing the team on. No reader of the unfolding drama of the Moses story fools themselves that he was doing any more than sitting and being held. He was spent. My reading of the charity's drama helped me to see that John was past tired, beyond verbal encouragement, and too far gone to enjoy a short restorative rest. It is a joy to tell you, though, that John returned to working in the charity sector elsewhere, advancing the cause of those in need.

There are many understudy analogies. In New York once, the Italian tenor Francesco Anile lounged in the green room of the Metropolitan Opera House in jeans and trainers, knowing he would not be needed. One last song in the performance of Verdi's Othello and the show would close. Francesco, practiced and ready, did not expect to be called upon again. But he was. In the final moments leading to the final act of the performance, the lead tenor began to lose his voice. Before a packed audience and to their amazement Francesco appeared in the middle of the cast. White trainers and blue denim jeans out of place for an Othello, his voice clarified the justification for his presence. That night he walked from backstage to centre stage - from understudy to star.

All productions have an understudy, someone who knows the lines and moves and can, at a moment's notice, stand in for the lead. An understudy is clear about what to do and has specifically been trained to deliver. In literature, a well-worn plot includes the use of a jealous understudy who will even kill the lead to get the part. They stand in the wings waiting to become centre of attention. Nothing could have been further from my thinking when John exited the stage that day. I remember being asked the direct question: "Do you want to take this on?"

Did I have a choice, and was there an alternative? Questions flooded my mind. Knowing there were money problems, I recognised the charity's survival included losing some staff. During the week, when this question was posed, I had some very powerful spiritual encounters. During my times of prayer, I received clarity of vision for the work at St. Paul's Centre. It was as though I was being moulded to the building and prepared for purposes not yet clear. On reflection, and with the benefit of twenty years' worth of experience, I can identify with the church's namesake, Paul. Standing before King Agrippa, the Apostle said: "The vision has never faded or left." As I will explain later, in those early days of leading the charity I received the much-needed encouragement to press on, encouragement that remained strong when circumstances taxed me.

Serious, honest, reflective consideration took place. Hours of poring over spreadsheets and bank statements, bills and briefing notes – all brought one word to the fore: bankrupt! For a brief time, I referred to this moment in our history as the St. Paul's Centre crash of '97, and it was a crash! A loss of confidence in us was looming on the horizon. I had a conversation with a Trustee who asked if I thought it was time to wind down the charity and hand over the keys. We talked of giving the building to another organisation. It took me some time to articulate how I understood the word bankrupt in our context. Yes, we had money problems. Yes, some hard and uncomfortable truths needed to be addressed, but this was beyond financial bankruptcy. We called a Trustees' meeting.

Listening to the conversation around the table, I realised that what we needed most of all was to pray. We were pooling our knowledge and gathering experience, we were applying valuable management principles and business speak to what I recognised as essentially a spiritual problem. One of my boldest statements, said with apologetic insecurity, came out: "If you don't mind me saying, I think our collective wisdom got us in this mess and we need a different kind of wisdom to get us out of it, so can we pray?"

We fumbled through our varied and unique ways of praying. Anglican formal language was linked to Pentecostal volume and the odd well-crafted evangelical lecture to God – presumed to be deaf and daft! I heard a voice. Not as you would hear a voice when half-awake, or a voice of madness that goes away with education or medication. This voice was clear, crystal like. The words I heard were simple and profound: "I put my foot on this corner of Crewe over 100 years ago, to reveal my presence. I am not lifting it for a debt of £21,000 but I will remove my all if I don't have your hearts." Don't, as some people do when I tell this story, rush off asking whether God has a foot, or which foot he was removing. That's not the point.

This all made sense of the word bankrupt; we were morally and spiritually bankrupt, more than we were financially bankrupt. Where was the prayer, where was the servant commitment? I recall turning and posing the question to those in the room, asking if they were fully committed in heart and soul to the work. That day our board changed. Soon after, folk moved on and we had a new Chairman. We developed a new sense of spiritual direction. These were days when you could feel the urgency of what we came to understand as the re-establishing of our faith and putting things right. I walked out of that room with a deep discomfort with the name 3Cs. A collective embarrassment about declaring ourselves Christian had, I believe, weakened us.

Statements of intent are not vision. Vision, the kind of which I speak, is buried deep in your heart and often the most difficult thing to articulate. Organisations need vision statements. Teams need vision statements, but above and beyond all of this we needed heart revelation.

If you ask me what our vision is I will reel off some well-thought-through and carefully crafted words. On the wrong day, I will reel off our penultimate vision statement. Yes, we have had a few. Over the years, with successive Trustees, we have attempted to modernise, update or restate in contemporary language what the vision is. Sometimes members of the team confuse the vision statement with the mission statement, or even the values of the organisation. Of course, they are all worthy of a place but pale into shallow tones against the crisp, vivid and bright colour of what I saw as the revelation of our purpose.

Like Paul the Apostle giving account before King Agrippa, my life's work has been the undeniable impression left by a powerful encounter. To me it is a soul-scar, reminding me of the encounter, begging to be traced from one end to the other, a dream in which to remain awake. Built in 1869, St. Paul's is a church that has heard the prayers of Christians through two world wars and numerous social and political changes. On one occasion, when showing a visitor around, this man walked over to the wall opposite the organ loft and rubbed his hands on the plaster work. They became instantly dirty from years of dust and the fact that this is now a furniture warehouse. "Can you feel that," he said in a dreamy, warm northern lilt, "the prayers of thousands of saints impregnating the brickwork." I had never really given that possibility any thought before. I mean, does prayer, which by nature is spiritual, penetrate bricks which are temporal, solid matter?

The morning following the boardroom encounter, before anyone had turned up for work, the sun weak, the light bright, I turned the key and walked to the far end of St. Paul's Centre. Resting on an uncomfortable settee, by choice to stay awake, I read my daily thought. My practice at that time was to read from *My Utmost For His Highest*, a book drawn from the heart of Oswald Chambers, an Army Chaplain in the First World War. Usually it takes two passes before my brain gets what he is saying. This morning, like many others, I am seated in the altar area of the church beneath the magnificent stained glass window, breathing in the atmosphere.

I had been troubled by a lack of clear vision in the charity's sense of direction or mission. The six-million-dollar question in my heart was: What am I here to do? Gazing at the walls and windows I closed my worn copy of *Utmost* and prayed.

Prayer is such a personal thing. Should we sit or stand, speak out or remain in silence? Everything will depend on where we first discovered prayer. Some churches I have been in seem to think God is deaf or low on understanding; others treat God as a mind reader – which I am certain is well within the gifts of Deity. So, in my individual and personal way I said: "What's it all about then, where are you taking me?" Now, it is important to remember that we generally don't expect an answer and if an answer comes, it is more likely than not, not what we want to hear.

To my surprise, I got a response! No deep voice or beardy stuff. Bear in mind that at this point I am seated under a magnificent stained glass window which sits above a beautiful wooden carved scene of the Lord's Supper, and all of this surrounded by old furniture. In fact, from where I sat, I could see old furniture piled as far as the end of the building thirty metres away. Then, gone as quickly as it arrived, I saw the room divided by a first floor. People stood or sat on the first floor and I sensed joy and fulfilment. Peace was on their countenance. Four steps lead purposefully, solidly, up. Each step bore one word on its side: Hope. Dignity. Confidence. Opportunity.

This sighting was not tangible in the sense that I saw it before my very eyes; I was not in a semi-conscious state like those in a trance. The experience of this vision was internal, and yet as real as the words on this page.

Nevertheless, hardly the Four Horsemen of the Apocalypse. Somewhere in all this is me, my friends and the books I have read, the fears I carry and on we could go, until the moment when, for me, I received this as a vision from God. Yes, I could be sceptical about stuff like that, too. My favourite verse in the Bible helps me to understand what happened that day: Faith is being sure of what we hope for and certain of what we do not see.

It is true, I did not see an actual floor with people on top that day, but so powerful was the image, it has never left me. You need neither faith nor a vision to share that image; just visit St. Paul's Centre and see it for yourself.

Over the subsequent days and weeks, I fleshed out this vision that no one else had seen or had imprinted on their soul. It may not rank with Moses or Elijah, and its significance is not global, but something grabbed me enough to keep going through two decades. If on that day, I had known the cost to me personally, I would have been like Peter the fisherman, in the courtyard the night before the crucifixion, denying that I had ever heard God's voice or been associated with Him. However, the impression of God in my heart, and the words hope, dignity, confidence and opportunity, have been the sustaining power in my life and that of the charity's to enable us to remain focused on our mission.

Forgive my presumption, but I suspect that like so many people you will be leaning into the future with expectation - hope. Our experience in those early days at St. Paul's Centre was an encounter with a community, one profoundly lacking aspiration. Working with many unemployed men, I would ask them what they hoped for in the future, where they saw their life in one, two or five years' time. Even thinking about tomorrow was a painful practice for many of them. I believed God was calling me to build the ground on which hope can be developed. Hope or aspiration are difficult to conceive when you have little sense of dignity, and so we knew we needed to learn to value people, to love them whatever it took.

This was not easy and there were not only days when we got it wrong, there have been years of getting it wrong. The team would change and with it the dynamic. We would keep building and rebuilding, always stretching, leaning forward, modelling what we want for others. We noticed that when people accepted their intrinsic value as a human being, their confidence grew. Well you know, without being told, the people who seize opportunities are confident, value themselves and believe in a future yet to come.

That day in 1997, when we recognised that the charity had problems, was a moment in time when we could have stood frozen in the light of what appeared to be debilitating circumstances. Confronted by cries of "Don't just sit there..." is usually the moment we want to take time out. If you have spent any of your life near the church you may well have heard sermons about the moment when God asks Solomon to name anything he wants, and he can have it. I once heard a preacher say we should always be ready for such a question. That just doesn't work for me. My answer today will not be what I want or need in a week, a year… I'm not sure that you can prepare for such a question. I would have said to God, "Can I have some time to look at my options?"

If I were to take anything away from the St. Paul's Centre crash of '97, it would be the words of a wise minister friend, Geoff Willetts, on the morning I had no idea which way to turn. Geoff said: "Don't do today what you can leave until tomorrow." Through kind and wise words, through reflection and self-examination, and through the sure knowledge that we are more apt to get things wrong than right, I learned not to let people or circumstances push me into a decision.

Most of life's challenges don't require a call to the emergency services. Looking back, I see not a crash; I see choices. We had the chance to walk away, abandon ship, leave the mess for others. But we chose the most exciting opportunity ever offered. We ran with a new vision and a sense of moral and spiritual direction. Not for a moment do I regret this.

## FLESH ON THE BONES OF VISION

For most of the charity's history, and certainly during the past 20 years, many of the people at St. Paul's Centre were long-term unemployed. Many times, I saw in the faces of men, beyond the worn lines and discoloured skins, troubled minds and deep sadness. They lived in clouds of emptiness. The same was true for much of the town's folk - aspiration was in short supply.

As one young person put it to my school teacher friend, Ben, "We don't want to do well, sir, or we'll have to leave town because that's what happens." Can you imagine living in a town where doing well means leaving your friends and family? Welcome to Crewe in the 1970/80/90s. That town, Crewe, was home to the most prestigious motor car builder in the world, a car that inspires millions globally to own one as a symbol of achievement. For us, that was a world away. Twice a day, five days a week, we delivered basic support in the form of beds and food to local poor families who lived in sight of that famous factory that produced the magnificent Rolls-Royce and Bentley motor cars.

Standing on the steps of the altar where countless thousands had knelt to receive the bread and wine in an act of intimacy and hope towards God, there were a group of volunteers. Holding a one pound coin aloft, I offered this challenge: "You could use this pound to buy a lottery ticket or a bus ticket to a college. In three years at college, you could gain a skill for life and possibly never be unemployed again. Or you could take your chances on the lottery." Not one of them went to college and none of them won the lottery! That was in 1997. Through sadness and frustration, I report that in 2017 many continue to choose a lottery ticket over finding work.

Back in the 90s, as I talked to those men, it became apparent they had no sense of a bright future. In churches, Christians often sing 'Strength for today and bright hope for tomorrow, blessings all mine, with ten thousand besides.' This is, of course, a song concerned with the theology surrounding the journey through this world and on into the next. My audience could not see beyond their present circumstances, indeed could not sense 'strength for the moment,' let alone the day. In short, they lacked hope. They lacked the ability to believe in, and therefore work towards, a future yet to be discovered. It was in that moment that the first rung on the ladder of my vision made sense - HOPE.

We needed to invest in an undiscovered future. We needed to promote in people a belief that life can be different, better, productive and even fun. There is a term we hear often from our governments, levelled at a specific group of people: wealth creators, people who are championed for their entrepreneurial prowess. Well, we became 'hope creators' with the emphasis not on championing the creators but the recipients. Simply put, it was not about us but those we serve.

Once we had found the sense of vision, the idea that we might find some mechanisms to put clothes on the skeleton of our vision became a consuming fire. My wife, Cheryl, and I began to press our minds into how we could focus and fire-up the disheartened and dysfunctional before us.

My mind was drawn to the approach, not always popular, of President Franklin D. Roosevelt's, in response to The Great Depression in the 1930s. He put people to work, gave them something to do and directed their minds to their hands. In a very small way, we knew this needed to happen at St. Paul's Centre. That busyness, in a way, would create space for folk to think beyond the moment in which they sat.

We noticed how much we all looked back to better times and want to be there again, but knowing that it wasn't as good as we thought. Black and white films with steam engines rolling through a junction - clickety clack, clickety clack - give off no smell or soot in our perfectly hazy memory. The terrible injuries sustained, and shortened lives, are not well promoted in the romance of memory. The town's rail heritage is a huge part of the local psyche and forms images of a golden era that never was.

Sat opposite me in my office was Brian. He was in his 60s, a local man who knew nothing other than the railways. "So, what do you want to do Brian?" I asked. "I want my old job back, it's what I did best," he replied. "What was that then, Brian?" He went on to describe his many years as a riveter at the rail works. I soon realised he was out of work because for too long his desired route back to work was a path barred by a no entry sign, which stated that the world had moved on. Brian was looking for a dignified end to what he saw as his working career. He had known nothing else and had no real desire to learn new skills. It struck me that being 60, when you have worked in an office or a less physically demanding job, may leave some resources for change and new vision, but pounding a hammer for eight hours each day for twenty years can leave you numb.

We learned that the fulfilment of our vision would have to be specific enough to hold the organisation together and broad enough to meet the needs of those we were to serve. The movement of furniture proved to be the perfect vehicle. There was something for everyone to do, and the task was endless – never complete.

In those early years, we collected around 10,000 items of furniture a year. It literally came in one door and out the other. Folk like Brian could rest with us, dream of steam engines, and be part of life. He never did find paid work but was enabled to have a dignified end to his thoughts of a working career. Brian taught us to not over think what we believed any specific person should do. Hope or aspiration in Brian's world was not the same in the world of others. It wasn't so terrible that he did not pick up a pay cheque again, and it may have been demoralising if he had been made to.

One morning, a guy called Tom rang the office and said: "I can't come in to work this morning as my wages haven't gone into my account. I'm going to the job centre to sort it out." Tom was 27, and unemployed drawing state benefits. Somewhere in his circle of friends and family he had picked up language that led him to believe unemployment benefit was a wage. I had not come across this phenomenon before. Here's the thing, Tom was a volunteer and rightly labelled what he did as work – in fact, he told everyone he worked at the 3Cs. He didn't get paid for this but it gave him a sense of identity. His work at St. Paul's Centre created a conversational anchor in the sea of his life to point to as his contribution. The state benefit, in his mind, was compensation for the work he did just like working in a factory and receiving a salary. So for Tom the words volunteering and work were interchangeable as were benefits and salary. I work, I get money and these two need no formal connection.

"What do you do?" is something that we are all asked by interested people at dinner parties, in pubs and in both private and public encounters. Wrapped in where our hands find work, is often thought to be our identity. It is not. Yet society, family and friends all look to the labour in which we find ourselves as a defining statement, a justification of our position or standing in society.

What we noticed was that Tom had lost a vital connection or understanding of the social model in which we operate. However productive or valuable the work a volunteer does in a charity, it is not the role of the state to pay a wage as compensation. Tom was young, and unlike Brian had a vast horizon of opportunity ahead. Our challenge in shaping the mechanisms to see our vision fulfilled had to include some element of push, or at least strong encouragement for Tom.

Through this early encounter with Tom, and the reflection generated by it, we recognised a burgeoning ethos that has kept us faithful to our sense of who, ultimately, we lean on to provide our direction and needs. As an organisation, we are Christian, and as a legal entity we are a charity, an arm of the church and not of the state. We recognise that there is a subtlety here which can cause blurred lines.

Tom forgot that it was his responsibility, ultimately, to fund his lifestyle through employment. He created in his world view a direct link and responsibility of the state with his labours as a volunteer - a link which did not exist. Over the years we have sought to avoid this ourselves. We do great work and make a huge difference to people. Hundreds have found a new independent, less state-dependent life through our efforts.

But we are not owed for this, nor have a right for compensation in the pursuit of fulfilling our vision. Each day I would remind myself and the team of the words of our first vision statement. Christian Concern wants to create a world in which we bring change, so we are responsible for finding ways to do this. When the local authority and the state withdrew funding, or grant aid, we could not see this as a loss of 'our right' to resources.

Around this time, we drilled down to specific tasks to be carried out and defined areas of responsibility. How could we let the Brians of the world rest and bring his working experience to a conclusion in a safe and supportive environment, and within the same environment bring firm supportive challenge and pressure to the Toms of the world?

In short, we broke the tasks down - and down again. For every action there was a lesson. We found the National Vocational Qualification system really helpful. To drive our thinking towards people and away from furniture we engaged in the Investor in People process.

Sat at an Investor In People conference, I looked up at the man peering out over the assembled audience with a picture of himself with Mount Everest in the background, he said: "I was not alone." Sir Chris Bonington was the guest speaker at my first business leaders' gathering. It was memorable and awkward. I had the cheapest suit and felt out of place until Sir Chris spoke. He described all the people that put him up the mountain, down to the bloke that got him the right kind of socks. He told of the friends who died attempting the mountain. One occasion, when he was within metres of the top, he turned back. He put this option to choose retreat as more important than daring to stretch for the unobtainable. If he had gone on that day, the weather front coming over would have taken his life. Pure gold in terms of vision and team building was the talk that day. He unfolded his very detailed step-by-step plan which started with a vision to stand on the top of the world.

A few days later, a new Trustee to the charity told me: "Stop dreaming vaguely and dreading precisely, and flip this thinking." He meant stop being precise about the things that prevent us doing what we want to do. At the same time, be precise about exactly what we wanted to do. In simple terms, stop talking about having a van to move furniture; tell me the make, model, colour and cost and set the date of delivery. The dreads disappear.

It was at this point we decided to have a detailed development plan. We specified what we wanted to do as a charity, and how we would achieve this. Whilst there is much that we could say about this, one thing became clear over the next two decades: we determined not to travel the path taken by many charities whose direction and vision are shaped and channelled in line with funding opportunities. We found funding to facilitate OUR vision; thus, we retained our independence.

At this point in our story, we knew who we were, and what we wanted to do. Every opportunity, including funding and partnerships, was questioned against our vision to ensure that no conflict or compromise of our independence took place. In the next chapter, the essence of that vision is revealed…

## HOPE

Creating hope in people is hard work because the failure rate is high and the pain can be very personal. We let each other down, disappoint and change our view of each other along the way. I remember one of the first men for whom I truly believed change for the better could happen. In an instant I saw a kind and soft man with an interest in others. Sitting at my desk, uncomfortable with the open-plan office setting, I stared at the document in my hands. Sentences and words poured from the page, all beyond my comprehension. I wondered who wrote the phrases, and who were they trying to impress? My early days in the world of charity brought me into contact with a vocabulary unfamiliar to many. A world within a world, a hidden language designed to keep others out, I thought.

"Would you like?" was a question that came from above that morning, a hand offering a cappuccino-flavoured chocolate. From head to toe he was covered in tattoos including a swastika on his neck. Just over six foot and less than ten stone wet through. Dave was a local man with more baggage than Heathrow airport. Taking the chocolate, I asked him to tell me what he was good at. A nervous smile spread across his face, head angled, almost listing as tall people often are when reaching down to the lower world of those under six foot. His was one of those apologetic looks, which suggested that he didn't think I would find any worth in him. He was wrong.

Pressing him some more, I discovered an interest in furniture restoration; so, I parked that knowledge. This is something you learn in leadership – collecting and parking knowledge or information. As one who struggles with overeating on occasions, I should discipline myself to recognise that what's in the cupboard is for later, and what's on the plate is for immediate consumption. Strategic thinkers and networkers do this all the time with information and ideas.

A few weeks after meeting Dave, I discovered a local 'under spend' in some European money the local council held. This is part of that charity speak I needed to learn; an under-spend. In parts of rural France men dream of finding a pig or dog who can sniff truffles at thirty metres; in charities, we dream of a fundraiser who can sniff an under-spend thirty days before it's recalled! This under-spend in question was for training and skills development for the unemployed. I found Keith, the local voluntary sector liaison officer, got the form, filled it in and cashed the cheque all in a week. Twenty years later and now retired, Keith is one of our volunteers.

Using some of the money, Dave and I built a woodworking workshop. It comprised twenty-five ex-NatWest Bank desktops, and some dodgy foam material for the roof. Bringing a vision from something in the mind to fruition demands action, and so we acted. This was a humble start and the focus was on the production of something inside the workshop, not the workshop itself. It was a cobbled together man cave.

And if I don't mention the electrics it won't be used in evidence against me! But it worked, and it started the ball rolling…

My next move was not to give Dave a job but the skills that would help him to believe in himself. Another key lesson in these early days of vision building was to hold the tension of beneficiary and benefactor. I wanted Dave to find a paid job and be proud of working and earning. The challenge was to build or create something that brought the vision I had for Dave to a place where other people in similar circumstances could benefit. This was not a permanent resting place for Dave; it was a watershed. He needed regular encouragement to lift his eyes to the horizon, and ultimately launch out into it.

Our experience at the charity has been that whenever we needed someone for a specific role, they always appeared. I advertised a job, paying a low salary, against the flow of some internal negative comments, mainly about who we could get for the money. The adage if you pay peanuts you get monkeys is an awful statement born of utter ignorance and a disregard for the intrinsic value of others who may choose to work for less.

Responding to my advert was Derek, a retired engineer who taught evening classes in furniture restoration at a local college. Derek and Dave were the perfect match for me because they fulfilled a vital link in building people up. Exposure to others from all walks of life, and their authentic personal journey meant that they arrived with a varied and long list of skills. Derek had climbed the ladder and enjoyed a senior position in Rolls-Royce before retirement. He was articulate, compassionate, professional and more qualified to do my job than I was. The contrast he brought could be seen in the new addition to the daily newspapers. It brought a smile to my face one day when I saw Derek's copy of *The Times* open at the crossword page, and *The Sun* open at a page with asterisks in place of a swear word. We had found a man with more knowledge and skills than time would permit to share. Derek had a real desire to impart or pass on what he knew. The creation of hope works best when we model what others less aspirational can value.

Over the years, I have found that talking about jobs and wages is quite low on the list of priorities for most people I encounter, even for the unemployed. Belonging and making a valued contribution in life are what make dreams more palatable and give them longevity. Winston Churchill is attributed with saying this: "We make a living out of what we get, we make a life out of what we give."

This appeared to be true of Derek. He proved that it is possible to find fulfilment in work and home life: to bring up children and invest in others. He shared the joy of knowledge and insight with Dave, revealing what Dave really craved for - his part in community. One day, I sat chatting to him and it became apparent to me that he did not know where he fitted into the puzzle of community groupings. We all need to be in community, be that within the family structure, at the bowls club, in church or at work.

It was beautiful to watch the mixing of skills and relationships in the workshop. In the teaching and learning involving how to cut material to shape and fit a seat cover, were blended many strokes of the soul, food for the future and ideas to run wild with. We found that working 'alongside' is much better than working 'on' a person. Despite the rhetoric of tabloid newspapers, most people have had enough of things being done for them or to them. One lesson drawn from the past twenty years, of engaging with the marginalised, is to never drift towards separating the deserving and undeserving poor. In our experience, much like the toddler taking its first brave steps, most people recovering or returning want a steadying hand, not an arm lock. In all my years at the coal face working with broken people, I met very few who wanted to be in the circumstances they found themselves.

So, what happened to Dave? He learned how to reupholster chairs, French polish and glue a broken gate leg table. Most importantly, he could look you in the eye and say that he could do those things. After a year, he left to work in London for a while in pubs, but not behind the bar. He travelled around reupholstering bar stools and seats. The next time you sit on a worn chair in a pub; be reminded that under your bum might be life changing possibilities!

Sadly, Dave died in 2014. What has not, indeed cannot die and remains indelible on my mind, is my memory of the first day of being greeted by him. He reached towards me, and my response helped shape the vision God placed on my soul – a vision of hope creation. The offer of a chocolate led to the charity developing a series of workshops including woodworking, cycle repairs and white goods engineering.

We use the words 'creating hope' because for so many people whose lives have been blighted by a reinforced narrative of 'you can't' or 'you will never,' the mere idea of an aspiration can be painful. Imagine being disappointed not by a failed attempt at achieving or reaching forward but at the base level of thinking you might fail. Creating hope for us was this: presenting someone with a way they could dare to have a go. We brought people like Derek and Dave together to show what could be. The beauty, and to some extent the mystery, is combination. Derek had not simply had aspiration, experience and a measure of fulfilment, but Dave had an interest at the time in what Derek could share.

Many, many times in our history people speak of replication, but every time we have recognised St. Paul's Centre is unique and the feeling folk have just before they say "Wow!" is drawn from the combination of time, place and spiritual presence. Over the years, I have often found myself saying to some of our folk, "You can't see it, but I see you running a shop, managing a factory, working for yourself…"

Like parents with great hope for their children, so the community at St. Paul's Centre has great hope for those we come to serve. In Dave, as in so many others, a stumbling block was simply a sense of unworthiness.

## DIGNITY

In 1505, Queen Anne of Brittany commissioned a court painter known as the Master of Antoine de Roche to produce a book for her daughter. The theme was biblical and included a picture of Adam and Eve, naked as in the biblical story. In recent times, the curator of the museum that held the work enlisted the help of the Department of Applied Mathematics and Theoretical Physics in Cambridge to restore the picture. They discovered a subsequent misguided owner many years later had commissioned 'dignity garments' to be added to the naked couple. The original painting was faithful to the biblical story recognising the context of the nakedness. Covering the couple to restore dignity, for what seemed like valid reasons, took the images away from their intended purpose. As one of my friends said of the Adam and Eve story, the problem wasn't the apple on the tree, it was the pair on the ground and their interference with God's set plan. It seems to me that in covering their nakedness the image their creator first held of them was lost, interfered with. The restoration of dignity happened when we could see them as their creator saw them. This was the very heart of our understanding of this challenge to restore dignity.

In that fleeting moment mentioned earlier, when at the altar, I was given four words; the second was all about the restoration of dignity. We recognised there was an image of us that is true in the Maker's eyes, yet so often lost. With very little thought in terms of planning and strategic thinking we became 'dignity restorers.' Like Dave in the previous chapter, and over time, we discovered that many of the people we encountered had layer upon layer of difficult circumstances and personal pain covering what we knew to exist underneath.

One of the privileges in life for me has been to work with my wife, Cheryl, who in turn worked with many of the people we met over the years. Never a scientific division, but in the main Cheryl focused on the women and I dealt with the men.

One young woman, Beverly, left a legacy we will never forget. Encouraged by Cheryl, she recorded in a weekly diary her journey as she experienced it. This was to be her aid to memoir, a list of tasks completed to help her build a truer picture of her life, not a false narrative born of the mental images she held of her unworthiness. This is a challenge when you have a poor education and sense judgment from those you hoped would bathe you in approval. Her English was a work in progress, but she knew what she meant and could read it back to Cheryl.

Working alongside Cheryl in the laundry and school uniform shop, she learned to read instructions and prepare the shop. In the early days, she was quiet and shy, often displaying, to the experienced eye, signs of past abuse and fear of men. We just loved her and treated her like a family member, which in our family meant using humour to challenge untidiness and sitting down to eat together as a way of holding meaningful conversations. Over many lunch times, Cheryl got to know Beverly, and not all was easy to hear. Then one day she wrote in her diary that St. Paul's Centre was the only place where she had been treated like a proper human being. She discovered she mattered and her voice could be heard; her life had value.

In so many ways, Beverly became the first real understanding for us of what it meant to restore dignity. The person whose dignity had been stolen and found again needs to feel and caress their new-found status, and Beverly did just that. She became vocal and engaging. She played practical jokes on us with no fear of upsetting us. In short, she relaxed in our company.

In one diary entry, she wrote the following: 'Tasks most enjoyed this week: Watching Cheryl get her knickers in a twist when I sorted the uniforms out.'

Her previous experience of a close relative becoming frustrated would have drawn tears of fear, not laughter. Cheryl's frustration caused Beverly no concern. These are what governments of all persuasions call 'soft outcomes'. These are not considered of monetary value in the people-changing market place. Such changes often leave people still too distant from being job ready – or economically non-productive. The truth is that without these changes in people they will never function well in family, community, employment or any other social role. This is not deep psychology or rocket science; in following the challenge of

Jesus to do unto others as you would have them do unto you. Dignity is restored. The image of the Creator comes back into relief. Over the years, I have met hundreds of people like Beverly and every one responded to authentic love.

Brokenness and dysfunction are words used frequently to explain or describe what we came to understand as a loss of dignity. There are programmes and skilful counsellors who ably lead people through the journey at the end of which can be found a measure of peace. I believe the value of our experience is found in the simplicity of finding something to do with the person and walk with them through it. Beverly helped sort, wash and prepare bedding packs for more than 300 poor families in her time with us. That was needed and was worthwhile. However, it provided a useful distraction from her own needs, and in working with Cheryl on these tasks trust was built. I believe Beverly discovered she could contribute and she was a valued part of the community.

Henri Frederic Amiel, a Swiss writer with a profound capacity of self-analysis, believed that how we conduct our lives is much more important than how we say we are going to live. It's not uncommon for many of us to recognise the benefit of having a morning jog, but many of us fail to get out and run. Talking about something is one thing, but learning new habits is everything and brings substance to life.

Through consistent reaffirmation and the facilitating of replaying that affirmation, Beverly developed the mental habit of thinking of herself as of worth. If you like, we sensed she changed her predisposition from feeling or believing in a profound lack of self-worth to a heightened sense of personal value. Amiel is quite right in suggesting that saying 'you have value' are words, whereas experiencing being valued is a changed state.

It would be wonderful to tell you that at St. Paul's Centre we valued everyone and held the line of restoring and enhancing human dignity all the time. We didn't. There were many occasions when the ugly side of our humanity came out and regrettably we failed. Deep in my heart - and this is shared with most of those in the charity - I believe no one is beyond rescue. Some of the characters we encountered over the years tested this to the limit and beyond.

One morning, moments before our new Chair of Trustees, Chris Demetriou, was due to arrive we had an incident that he will never forget. Each morning we stand together and say a prayer after dividing up the day's work. We choose who is out on which van. Decision made, and prayer said, I walked to the office. As I did so I heard the words "I'm not taking that ***** out on my van," from one of the drivers. Wrestling with racing heart and swelling tongue, I turned and blasted the driver.

No swear words, or particularly derogatory terms, but cold unambiguous hard words. I felt incensed that one of the people we considered vulnerable, a terrible term for someone with learning difficulties, was being rejected – called by callous words. For a brief millisecond, I identified with Jesus as he had cleared the money lenders from the temple. That said, I didn't turn any tables over.

Our Chair of Trustees arrived at the front of the building and one of the office staff brought him to the rear where I was ejecting the driver. He was shouting at me and I was telling him he had no place with us: "You're the lowest of the low, and Kevin is worth ten of you," I was ranting. He went on to threaten me and I responded with that terrible male testosterone: "In your dreams." I think this is where the correlation with Jesus and the temple clearance and Rob ended.

I locked the gate and turned around to see Chris, our new Chair, smiling at me. He was kind and completely understood the situation. But here's the truth: that driver was not worth ten of Kevin, and he was not the lowest of the low. That day, I was reminded of the need to hold the sanctity of human dignity for all. However difficult a person is, on our journey we have learned that we are human too. It is within our capacity to remove as well as restore dignity. As a footnote of sorts, you may like to know that we made friends and the driver continued his work after a hand shake and some humble words were exchanged.

It was our privilege to be there when many others had the light of realisation come on. Through laughter and tears, the balance of the community at St. Paul's Centre cleared a path for love and acceptance to edge some towards a greater appreciation of the value God placed upon them. They rose above the cruelty of circumstance and learned to look out from a position of strength. It would be unfair to give lists of names, but yours is the work of imagining the countless men and women over thirty years who walked into St. Paul's Centre with head down and heart convinced of their lack of worth. Ours has been the privilege to see them walk out, head up and with a new song in their heart. A former worker at St. Paul's Centre, and lifelong supporter, once used the phrase "It is as though God stoops down, lifts our hearts and gently strokes them."

It may sound formulaic but we discovered that having a vision for the future in which I am competent at something and in which the debilitating sense of unworthiness is absent equips people emotionally to take a risk and try something. For Beverly, failure was not the issue; rejection was. We work on the delicate balance of encouraging folk, but often using stabilisers so that a fall is less painful.

## CONFIDENCE

There can be few professions in which the words 'no confidence' appear with such frequency as in politics. If the British Prime Minister appears on the steps of 10 Downing Street to declare: "The minister for kerb stones has my full confidence," it is a sure sign that the minister is on their way out. We place great store in being confident in another person, so much so that often they nosedive, falling under the weight of pressure to fulfil the expectation of another's confidence in them. For me to say that I am confident in your ability is one thing, but for you to be confident in your own ability is another thing entirely.

When we hear someone say "I can't," we have learned to recognise that often this is used to disguise the fear of failing.

As a child, I had a terrible incident in my life when my father genuinely attempted to build my confidence. Unfortunately, this lesson involved me being forced to fight two boys who stole my bike. My father wanted me to retrieve it from them. I simply could not win. The next time my bike was stolen, my father was the last person I turned to for help.

Our confidence can often become knocked when in the presence of confident people. Studies and reports are regularly published about low confidence leading to all manner of social ills. The strength of our confidence is a human condition that some of us simply cannot seem to alter, and may not need to. We have all seen the brother and sister raised in the same environment with identical care and nurture. One picks up a bike and rides without a wobble, the other never looks steady on two wheels. The confident child with no wobble falls off the bike, takes a little coaching, then gets back on the bike. They just get it. The wobble leaves.

Sometimes, we need people who can overcome a wobble, to help us work with others, or even to further assist their own return to daily life. One man springs to mind. His voice was southern, sounding as though he originated from somewhere near London. "My doctor suggested I come along," he said. We walked around the centre and I saw his eyes glint at the wood workshop. He engaged with Raymond with fluidity and ease. I could tell this was a man used to being in control. In fact, Ted had worked for a multi-national organisation as a buyer. His job had involved travelling the world and meeting very interesting people. Like Derek, he read *The Times*. Ted had cared deeply about his work, but not as deeply about his health. This had led to a heart attack and some enforced unemployment. He did not qualify for benefits. Ted was no different to the other folk around the centre. He had lost confidence and needed to see an alternative future that at that moment was beyond his view.

Having shown folk at St. Paul's Centre that an alternative future could exist and, in some instances, having restored their sense of personal worthiness, we moved into the area of the vision which is about building. Working with people who, for many reasons, think they cannot do or face something, required us to take what fledgling confidence they had and build upon it. Speaking about opportunities and change to people with little or no confidence was difficult. I am clear in my mind that overwhelmingly the people we helped, and those spoken of in this book, would not want to see themselves at St. Paul's Centre as clients, recipients or beneficiaries. This is a great place to start, and a platform for them to develop confidence in doing for others just as they would like to have done for them. Many would see their time with us as a contribution to the wider community. They gained and grew in the process of giving to others.

From a world of millions of pounds and pressure to deliver, Ted brought into our little workshop thirty years of high-level strategic thinking. He joined Karl, a recently redundant bank manager who was passing time. The in-joke was that we were creating a safe house for retired men hiding from wives with long lists of DIY jobs to be done around the home.

One afternoon, I visited the workshop to see how things were going only to be met by a production line of bird boxes and tables. Off-cuts of timber were organised into sizes and a design area had been created for ideas to use the smaller pieces. In my heart, I loved it; in my head I knew it had to stop. It was like the thrill of being on a fast train. You put your head out the window and scream with the flush of excitement until you discover the driver is not there and you are on a runaway train. The thrill ends and the panic sets in because the outcome could be anything - and you can't control it. Welcome to what it can sometimes be like running a charity.

I spoke gently to the guys about the purpose of their time volunteering, that it was to help them and to help some of our less able folk learn new skills and enjoy making something. In truth, Raymond and Geoff, two of our adults with learning needs, were in league with the would-be billionaires. In my mind the workshop was not about the products that we produced. If a bird box was unfit for habitation, and no self-respecting Tweetie Pie would be seen dead in it, that was fine if the maker of the box had enjoyed making it, learned from the making and was proud of what they made. These guys had implemented a quality control system which included a pile of rejects that needed to be reworked. "Where is this leading guys?" I asked. It was at this point I came face to face with myself.

My own words were fed back to me. "Wouldn't it be great to find an outlet for the bird boxes and tables, maybe a garden centre? We could have a stand which we restocked once a week," I had mused. It is true; I did say that because that's what I do – I dream out loud. In my defence, I had in mind a small local gardening centre, whereas these guys were thinking B&Q or Home Depot in the United States.

Both those guys brought boundless energy and vision to a small part of the charity. They rested with us during a moment of unplanned pause on the wheel of stress-filled careers. The journey of confidence re-building with us in their context was about downscaling activity to a manageable level; a refuelling if you will. Why didn't I use them and their wealth of experience and contacts in the commercial world in our fundraising or strategic activity? Surely they could have helped to develop the charity and bring sustainable income streams? Because that is not what they needed. What they needed was to keep getting up and going out to work, to be part of the adult world. They needed not to stop so completely that they would not get moving again.

The fear of failure and rejection drives many of us to resist having a go. A 51-year-old man sat in my office unsure of where his future lay. I asked him to tell me about his dreams, what he really wanted to do. Moments earlier he had been standing arms round my shoulders and sobbing. His 6'3" heavy frame was all but crushed and he was facing the deep, black hole of zero confidence. I said take a seat mostly because I needed a breather.

My line of invitation was along the "don't narrow your horizons" line of thinking. "I have got a dream," he told me, "I always wanted to play professional football." Calmly, I looked at his more than oversized waistline, greying hair and nicotine-stained fingers, and said: "Some dreams just aren't right for us; what's your second choice?"

I learned over the years that untruths set people up for a fall that could be avoided. In helping people build confidence it became hugely important to be realistic. Honesty can clear the desk of impossible projects and leave you with that which can be achieved. To my six-year-old granddaughter, I can say: "You can do whatever you want." She has time to work at it and very few restrictions. To my 80-year-old mother, I need to say: "You can do what you want to with the limited time and capacities you have."

We can count more than fifteen women who over the years have worked, both paid and as volunteers, at St. Paul's Centre for whom the journey was all about the rebuilding of lost confidence. In the main, these were women who had chosen or been engineered into staying at home longer than necessary after the children had gone to school. On multiple occasions, I heard "I just want to meet some adults, and preferably without prams or screaming kids".

One lady, beautiful in spirit, who was in a challenging relationship, told me how entering St. Paul's Centre in the morning liberated her to feel herself, free and without concern for her words. The atmosphere at home was tense. I remember watching her slow progress to the door each evening and recognised that I left to go to a less stressful environment; she had the opposite experience.

Another kind and generous woman who we employed had been away from the world of paid work for thirty years. She came to us nervous and lacking in confidence. She feared making mistakes and was like a child the first day at big school. The atmosphere, relaxed and full of humorous incidents on the delivery vans settled her. In the months to come, we learned that this was one tentative step in a series towards a new and independent life. She achieved that new life within the year.

Our experience with the younger generation is similar. They arrive shy and quiet and leave confident and engaging. One of our projects is a cycle refurbishment workshop, in which we select each year a young person with a lack of direction to work with us. Invariably, they have confidence issues. One of these young men, Josh, typified what we are about. Before his 'trainee' year was up, he could re-spoke a wheel whilst throwing sarcasm around the workshop. He arrived with a CV that said chip shop assistant, and left to take a job with a national cycle supplier. He didn't keep this job because his aspiration, sense of purpose and confidence grew such that he went on to university to take a degree.

We learned that whether a person was 16 years old or 60, at the entrance to life's great journey or at the close of it, the absence or loss of confidence is crushing. It was strangely frightening for those in their 50s and 60s looking out on a shorter horizon. In the early days, my focus was more on the younger generation, to whom I spoke much about college, training and trades, but soon learned what a great leveller low confidence and limited opportunities can be. We discovered the life-giving buzz that anyone of any age or academic standing can gain came from mending or making something, and from helping those less well-off.

The mature men in the workshop, the women on a new journey or coping with the disappointment of their current one, and young Josh in the cycle project all benefited from activity in a space that encouraged the growth of confidence. Each, in turn, took their new-found fledgling confidence and moved on to grasp what was already before them but with fresh eyes.

## OPPORTUNITY

My grandson, Kudzai, and I love to sit and watch a film together. This usually involves some form of food treat, a blanket and invariably missing the normal bed time slot. When his mum was young, it used to be endless re-runs of *Father of the Bride*, something I'm still waiting to be with her. With Kudzai and I, it's usually something more far-fetched, and one such film is *Evan Almighty* starring Steve Carell and Morgan Freeman. In the movie, Carell is a modern-day Noah, building an Ark, and Freeman is God. In a moment of despair and confusion, Noah's wife heads out of town embarrassed by his public antics intent on leaving him. The family is set to break up.

Morgan Freeman, disguised as a waiter and serving her, asks why she is so sad. The conversation leads to Freeman pointing out that earlier she had prayed for patience and for the family to stay together. Freeman says: "God doesn't give us patience. He gives us circumstances in which to exercise and grow in patience." We can only discover our gifts and talents through use. Whilst contrived for entertainment, the truth in this exposé of human nature is that challenges can be embraced as opportunities to grow and develop. Opportunities to prove what we hope for are possible in some form. In the film, Mrs Noah returns not to a changed situation but as a changed person. She embraced the opportunity to keep the family together.

Our challenge as a charity was to find ways to enhance the opportunities that existed for our folk. To encourage them to see from a different standpoint. Many times, at St. Paul's Centre we hear people share how they have tried it, and they can't do it, or last time they tried something this or that happened. We had to learn to place them in front of an opportunity as a different person, with a new view of themselves, and to see an opportunity as just that - and not as a negative challenge. It was fascinating to hear young men from poor working class backgrounds talk of job interviewers, suggesting that they were trying to catch them out and trip them up with hard questions. The mentality we encountered was one of seeing a process of selection always from the perspective of the 99 who don't get selected, rather than the one who does. This narrative of expected rejection and disappointment in some ways altered the meaning of the word opportunity for them.

The benefit system in the UK does not help because the focus is on justifying how many applications you, the unemployed, make to qualify for unemployment benefits. It's not the best system, and some would like the system to change to reflect quality and not quantity. Our role was to get the folk we supported out of the system and into a new frame of mind. To our advantage has been the fact that we are not the government, and our role has no element of policing.

We learned that this is a team effort dependent upon the input of several layers of people. To watch a cycle race without paying attention to the internal dynamics is to miss that it is a team sport. Everyone in the team has a unique skill, which is called upon to get other team members close to the finish line. The team can spend hours pushing and fighting fatigue to place one of their fellow teammates at the front of the pack for the final sprint. There comes a moment when the hill climbers and slow finishers peel off having presented the rider in front an opportunity to win. What they can't do, or indeed are not asked to do, is to cross the line for them. Paul the Apostle spoke to the church about focusing on the goal set before them. We found our challenge to be focused around gently, but firmly, helping folk to look beyond the perceived hurdle - to see the prize.

"It's not the fault of the baby," said the teenage girl. Sitting in a small meeting room discussing the topic of the day, I found myself navigating through some giggles mixed with serious comment. A local school teacher running a Christian Union had brought his pupils to St. Paul's Centre for a visit. Mostly girls aged 13 with a keen interest in the topic that filled the local news – teenage pregnancy. We debated the issue of very young girls becoming pregnant, and some lightness came into the discussion. Dressed too mature for her years, and with a cheeky self-confidence, one of the girls commented: "It could be one of us." In unison, they all craned their necks to one girl and said in a wise grandmotherly way: "It could be you." She looked away. In a flash, I pierced the discomfort in the room, and exclaimed: "So we have moved the discussion onto responsibility and culpability." Following their puzzled expressions, I explained that we had drifted into blame and judgement which then led to a wonderful and memorable conversation out of which came an amazing insight from a sensitive and thoughtful young girl. "But sir, it's not the baby's fault - it doesn't get to choose."

From this wise and insightful comment came a project that ran for over a decade and met the needs of more than 200 newly-born babies whose mums were teenagers and still considered to be children themselves. No suited men or focus groups; no funding applications or public appeals. There was no start date or project launch. These young girls asked their families and friends to sponsor them to walk around the town. They bought ten plastic boxes and filled them with quality baby clothes and two presents, a soft toy and a first book. These boxes were designed by those young pupils as the baby's first welcome to the community. Filled with practical and simple things, the soft toy and the book were to give them the opportunity to enjoy and learn. During one conversation, most of which was driven by the young people, it was decided an important message for this baby was for them to be inspired to discover they were not a mistake but a wonderfully intended being in a world that wanted them to succeed.

This word 'opportunity' became, in the early days, a powerful driver to enable us to be courageous in finding ways to put people in front of the net - as a football manager might say. It seemed to me that the lack of progress made by some of the people we met was down to a lack of opportunities and too many knocks.

The *Rocky* films are not actually accurate or true; a human being can only recover so many times. We hear songs on the radio that portray the experience of so few of us when it comes to overcoming knocks and moving forward. In 1997, around the time we were developing the vision and recognising just how hard it was for some people to move forward, the band Chumbawamba brought out a catchy song with the refrain "I get knocked down but I get up again, you're never going to keep me down." Getting up again happens in the movies and in song more often than it does in a small northern town in the UK.

Collecting some school items from our uniform re-use shop with her daughter, a distraught and frightened mother shared her pain with Cheryl. The uniform would soon not fit, as her daughter would shortly be needing maternity clothes. Through soft, apologetic and painful words this desperate woman articulated with limited vocabulary that she had another daughter at home who was already eight months pregnant; this mother seemed to have nothing in life but knocks and worry. With so many teenage pregnancies at that time in our town, you would be forgiven for thinking there was something in the water!

The Crewe water, however, was not the problem. Over the next few weeks we found for this growing family cots, prams, baby clothes and of course the baby's first present – a welcome box. The great challenge here is to avoid the easy slide we make into thinking that such issues will be dealt with by someone else – because they won't be.

We sometimes drift into discussions about fault and blame. On other occasions, we place the responsibly of dealing with complex social issues at the feet of the government. However, blame and passing the buck is not the route we at St. Paul's Centre chose to take.

Over the years, I have learned to filter out those well-intentioned comments that portray an over simplification of the complex circumstances that lead to teenage pregnancies or family dysfunction. Whilst I may personally believe that a child should be born to a happy couple devoted to each other, with savings and good jobs, and only bringing a baby into the world in a planned and organised way, life is not like that.

Interestingly, Jesus himself had an unusual entrance to the world. Joseph needed a serious chat with an angel to take up the challenge and Mary was no more than a child – they would have qualified for one of our baby welcome boxes. They, of course, got three with much more expensive gifts! Closer to home, my own daughter brought into our family a beautiful and balanced grandson that any grandfather would have wanted or prayed for. It didn't happen inside wedlock, and his father and mother failed to hold a relationship together. The experience of leading St. Paul's Centre has taught me that ideals are less important than relationships, and that very few negative circumstances are beyond turning.

As things in the centre grew and dealing with people became consuming we needed help. In terms of the school uniform recycling project, which later became the Whole Child Centre, help came in the form of two women, both called Chris. Just occasionally, we are privileged to meet and spend part of our life's journey with people of authentic enthusiasm and joy. Both these women had more energy than ten men. Chris C was a powerhouse of positive energy, and Chris L made me feel exhausted just watching her work. Over the years, I have met hundreds of well-meaning people who say they only have a few hours to give, and often this is linked to comments like "I'm not really very good at much." They are very rarely accurate in their own assessment.

There are many apocryphal or misrepresented stories of Francis of Assisi, words he never said. Let me risk adding to those with a twist on one of his wonderful statements. "Tell people God loves them and if you really have to, use words." In our experience at St. Paul's Centre, most people have no problem hearing kind words. The problem is experiencing kindness. That we care does not change their circumstances;

that we act does. Like so many we have worked with, most of us need to feel. Yes, feel the proximity of authentic people - and people able to inspire a vision of better circumstances, people able to fan into flame the courage to reach forward and dare to take hold of a new way of living. At St. Paul's Centre, we have attempted to be those very people.

## COLLEAGUES AND FRIENDS

Strolling through the door and taking what seemed like an age, Steve came into our lives. He offered a greeting in the form of a hand to shake. Dry, hard and iron-like to the touch, his hand wrapped around my softened office-worker's hand. Standing six feet tall, a couple of inches above me, he somehow appeared as a giant, powerful and rooted to wherever he stood. Where we differed mostly was in width; this is a man who turned sideways to pass through the average door frame. To the judging or less discerning eye, standing before me was a man to be feared, perhaps respected. Politeness and self-preservation on my part dictated that I did not stare, let alone read the tattoos that covered his arms, but curiosity gained the upper hand and my eyes left his to read where the ink had long dried.

Steve was a man you took a liking to, not instantly, but soon after. Family names and a favourite football team creatively and colourfully written on his skin spoke of pride and loyalty. Years of playing football in tough local leagues, and occasional door work for pubs, had placed a quiet confidence in the way he carried himself. This was a man to have as a friend, and not an enemy.

Sent by his wife, Chris, a volunteer at the centre, he was there to "get her off my back" he told me. Later, he confessed his intention had been to work for a morning and then clear off, hoping this would satisfy his wife.

For some time, his life had been chaotic, and work was not presenting itself. Days followed by weeks of unemployment meant a steady slip into surviving life without work. The odd bit of cash helping a friend out, and creative accounting from Chris, put food on the table and the latest Portsmouth football shirt on Steve's back. A set of twin daughters had followed their first child, also a daughter. This was not the full extent of the family. Walking into their living space, I was met by the softest Staffordshire Bull Terrier, a very slow tortoise, noisy parrot and fish tank. They were all squeezed into a small house on a prominent corner of a local housing estate. It was amazing that Steve hadn't been desperate to get out of the house for a few hours a day.

There could not have been a better time for a man of Steve's stature, temperament and personal situation to arrive at St. Paul's Centre. The Kosovan crisis was growing, and we were spearheading a town-wide response. Unboxed and unlabelled food had been flooding in to our warehouse, and not a date checked on a tin. One afternoon, before Steve had arrived, I had stood alone at the gate of the building receiving bag after bag of food. The rear of St. Paul's Centre faces onto a 500-space car park, formerly terraced houses, the other side of which stood the largest supermarket in the town. At the time, the town's folk had little choice but to park and shop right here at our back doors.

Responding to the newspaper challenge I had set the town, local people spent one pound on filling a plastic shopping bag with flour, rice, sugar and tins of tomatoes. Having loaded their own shopping into nearby cars, they walked the 100 or so yards to make their offering. Some days, bags piled up so much that we asked passers-by to help carry them in. The altar of the church was cleared of furniture and it became the food storage area. An army of volunteers did what they could, but it was overwhelming and food spilled from burst bags all over the floor.

One day I had a look of despair on my face, and Chris said that her husband was at home watching TV and doing nothing. This is the part where I would like to say that "having committed the needs we had to the Lord, I awaited an answer to prayer…" Well, in those long, busy and physical days, I learned to commune with God through nods and winks. No flowery language was needed; if God is God then God knows our needs, I thought. In situations such as those we encountered, prayers were fired off continuously and answers came just as quickly. Paul the Apostle spoke out of a pressure hard to bear, giving us the apt comment "We are hard pressed on every side, but not crushed; perplexed, but not in despair…." Of course, his situation was different, but the words still applied. Over the course of our time, we learned at St. Paul's Centre that there is a specific match for our needs. We discovered that not just anyone will do, it must be the right person. Offers of help, however kind, are not always wise to take because they may become a cause for prayer rather than the answer to one.

Steve was not an answer to our prayer; he WAS the answer. His commitment to give a half day's work developed into a full-time paid job and a lifelong friendship. His presence evoked the feeling you get when involved in a road accident and the emergency services turn up. A sigh of relief flowed through my tense body, reducing my heart rate and restoring calm to my panicked internal system. Over the next few weeks we received, weighed, labelled and sent more than 100 tons of food to hungry Kosovars we would never meet. It was a huge operation, and one day the haulage company we were using became difficult over concerns that we had no forklift trucks to load the lorry. Loading by hand, they thought, would take hours and, as the haulier said, time is money. We eventually agreed that the first hour of loading time would be free and a heavy financial penalty for every 30 minutes following.

One Sunday morning, I asked the minister of a local church, West Street Baptist Church, where Steve and Christine had begun attending, if I could speak. Many of the congregation were aware of our efforts and had dipped in and out with help. By now, I had learned not to offer the negative to people you want help from. "We have more than exceeded the food collection for the Kosovar refugees. Some of those refugees are sat with us this morning," I said, gesturing to a couple called Genti and Adelana, who smiled back. "Tomorrow morning, we need to load the food on a lorry." I went on to explain that the driver had a long journey ahead and appealed for help for one hour at the start of the day.

Just as the streams of people donating food had arrived, so the loading volunteers came. Teenagers to octogenarians snaked from the temporary store in the chancel through the centre to an empty, long, flat-bedded trailer parked at the gate. Steve climbed onto the lorry with the driver and one other giant-like form of a man. Box after box streamed its way to the lorry's side. Layer after layer of food boxes grew up until ten feet tall and filling the span of the space available. The lorry was three quarters full, with no sign of abatement, and the driver asked for a rest. Tea in hand, he leant against the one hundred and thirty-year-old church wall and watched what he described as a "well-oiled machine."

There is no end to the resilience and determination of a group of people committed to the welfare of others. Once the imagination of what could be overtakes the reality of what is, all limits seem to be removed. Steve was one of a line of amazing people God brought into our midst. Each one helps us to see what lies at the heart of St. Paul's Centre. Observing one life moved sufficiently to act, and motivated to change things, is a fulfilment of what John Ashe intended. As he travelled to Euston station in London in 1865, asking for money to build a space for local people to encounter God, he could well have had Steve in mind.

During the years that followed, Steve and I had some great adventures. Having driven cars for years on a motorbike licence, we helped upgrade it to a full driving licence – thus enabling him to drive our vans. For a season, Steve became the second in command and discovered in management a new-found dignity. His demeanour transformed, his horizon broadened. Once, when a member of the team was heard complaining that I kept changing the goalposts, Steve defended me. He said: "You're wrong, Rob doesn't change the goalposts, he lengthens the pitch." In those days, we were racing forward towards a vision of experience, not a specific destination. The plans changed by the hour. We would try something one way, and if it didn't work we moved on. This was not the way most people had worked; they were used to a slower pace with a deeper level of communication. Steve was one of the few who seemed to grasp the broad idea, and was adventurous enough to have a go.

I mentioned adventures, and there were plenty. We became friends with an Armenian doctor who lived locally and worked at the nearby hospital. He asked for help to transport some medical equipment that had been donated to his cause. A most resourceful man, with connections everywhere, Ara had a built-in radar for anything medical going for free. Honing his skills as a surgeon in Beirut, and now working in the UK, he travelled to his motherland annually to perform operations. When equipment became available he bagged it and sent it home where he was helping to build a hospital.

We agreed to help, and reversing up to a loading bay in the service area of the hospital we understood the collection to be of a small X-ray machine. Our vehicle had a weight restriction, and a tail-lift with limited capacity. This was a furniture van used to carrying wardrobes and beds. "It's over here, lads," said the porter, pointing to what appeared to be a contestant on Robot Wars. Wrapped in plastic, the arm stood six feet tall, and the diameter of a medium frying pan. This was fixed to a triangular base of a similar size to a dining table, but slender at the top. It was solid looking, and shouted "I'm heavy" at first glance!

With Ara's X-ray equipment on board, Steve and I drove to the airport early in the morning to miss the traffic and make it there and back in a day. The lorry was full but comfortable to handle. We sensed an excitement about what we were delivering. It was medical equipment bound for landlocked Armenia. He recognised the significance of what we were doing in terms of what the equipment would achieve for some of the poorest people in the world. Armenians are in many ways a forgotten people. Within 300 years of Christ's death, the nation of Armenia adopted Christianity as its official religion. They were the first to do this and have remained true to the faith since. These are a group of people who have known suffering and isolation. In 1915 the Ottoman authorities systematically rounded up and killed one and half million Armenians.

The subsequent diaspora created Armenian communities around the world, including the group living in the UK of which our friend Dr. Ara is one.

Turning onto Kemble Airfield, near Cirencester, we recognised a row of small planes - mostly Cessna aircraft. I turned the lorry towards the control tower and was waved to slow down and pull in. The man we met introduced himself as David and explained that he had been waiting for us. Drawing the vehicle alongside a hanger, I parked and climbed out. He asked if we would like some breakfast, to which we agreed. As we walked towards the control tower, below which was a small café, David then asked if we would like to go up in a plane. We nodded like excited children. He also asked if we had flown before. I confirmed my experience and looked at Steve. He casually looked up and said, "I used a lift in a high-rise block once." David stopped, turned around and said, "We'll eat after."

Within minutes Steve was at the controls, and I was sat in the back. David wanted to give him a unique experience. Chris and the girls found the tale hard to believe when we returned to Crewe. In the space of months, Steve had gone from unemployment and daytime TV pilot, to full-time work and piloting a plane, albeit for thirty minutes.

In sharing these precious memories, I am drawn to the conclusion that however well-planned and executed our recruitment programmes are, seldom do we find jewels like Steve through such means. The experience of discovering and working with Steve strongly enforces the notion that our journeys are more fully packed with excitement when we dare to be different and try new things.

During many adventures with Steve, we found a respect and trust that enabled us to achieve. We learned the true nature of each other's character allowing one to release and support the other at various times with various tasks. The death of my father was one such occasion. For all the obvious and complex circumstances when a person dies suddenly, one day, in the middle of a very busy development and without warning, I handed Steve the keys to the whole charity. "My dad just died, I need to leave," I told him. Without any questions, or a show of sudden anxiety at the responsibility he had just received, he simply said: "Leave it with me, it'll be okay here." I didn't return for a week and didn't need to.

There were many, many more characters like Steve. Men and women whose lives converged with ours. People who emerged from a slip road in life onto our motorway. They joined us in the lane that most suited them for that moment in their personal history. Each one left a mark, or a place where their presence was felt.

Rubbing my hand along an internal stud wall, I can feel the raised nail that Raymond, one of our vulnerable adults, hadn't fully knocked in. Elsewhere, my eyes fall on a patch of paint work, a little thin, where a Bentley Motors' apprentice, on loan for a day, had stretched the tin too far. And resting on the mezzanine floor, spider-like, is a racking system for storage. To the unknowing eye this is just warehouse stuff - metal and wood. To those of us around at the time it went up, the sight reminds us of Colin.

## FAITH AND LIFE'S ANCHOR

Work at St. Paul's Centre has taken us on many fascinating journeys, some quite literally to the other side of the world. Standing at the check-in desk to catch a flight to Tirana, the capital of Albania, Cheryl and I had a palpable excitement. Surrounding us were the sounds of other nations; costumes that spoke of cultures vastly different to our own. My internalised conversation circled around the amount of baggage one family had. I wondered what they would say to mitigate the excess baggage if they were challenged. They moved slowly towards the front desk.

Cheryl and I held our tickets and passports tightly. Apprehension dwelt within us, a recognition of flying to a country close to a war zone. Some of our friends and family thought us irresponsible, and certainly naïve. Watching a loved one taking a risk, or moving adventurously through life, is never easy. My mum made that clear. The words of Oswald Chambers interrupted my dreaming: "Every man is made to reach out beyond his grasp."

Hours earlier we had left Hannah, our youngest daughter, with my mother and boarded a bus to Heathrow Airport. We were bound for a small village in Albania called Derje. Our aim was to establish a link between the community in Crewe and those living in Derje.

It was early morning on Thursday, March 25, 1999, and we were moments from boarding our flight. We inched forward; the movement was welcome. "NATO closed the airspace over Europe," I overheard a man saying. Although well-planned and choreographed, we passengers were the last to be informed. All air traffic was grounded whilst NATO launched an air campaign named Operation Allied Force.

Flashing letters that read 'DELAYED' appeared against all flight numbers, including ours. We were utterly deflated. My adrenalin was

St PAUL'S CHURCH, CREWE

E.T.W.D.

Aug 88

# LEASE OF LIFE AT DISUSED CHURCH

A REDUNDANT church in Crewe is poised to become a Christian-based community centre and could also become a new home for the town's Dutton Institute.

The Chester Diocesan Board is recommending the Church Commissioners to transfer St Paul's Church at Hightown, which closed for worship in November 1986, to Crewe Christian Concern to be used for a variety of community purposes.

Among the activities that Christian Concern plans to house at the 119-year-old church is a creche for two-and-a-half to five-year-olds in conjunction with Cheshire County Council, use for adult education, and use as a head-quarters for the Relate marriage guidance council.

Other uses envisaged include

making it the headquarters of the Dial-a-Ride scheme which provides transport for disabled people, using the schoolroom as a 'drop-in' centre for the unemployed, and also setting up a photographic workshop and ceramic studio there.

Crewe and Nantwich Borough Council was expected to give support at a meeting of the community services committee yesterday afternoon. The council is suggesting the scheme could also incorporate the Dutton Institute, whose present premises in Prince Albert Street have become badly run down.

## Community

Set up in the 1930s, aim of the Institute is to provide club recreation for unemployed people.

The plans for the church have been welcomed by the Rev Colin Alsbury, whose All Saints parish encompassed St

Paul's.

He said: 'The Diocesan Board have been looking at alternative uses since the closure and this seems a very good package.

'While the use for religious services has gone it is will still be used to benefit the community and the Christian link is staying.

St Paul's was built by the old Railway Company in 1869 to help serve the people who came into the area to work on the railways and at one time its vicar was Canon Arthur Webb, brother of the Railway Company's chief engineer Frank Webb.

It closed for worship because redevelopment of the town centre removed many of the nearby homes. The choir stall and the imposing East window will be retained while parishioners have visited Holy Trinity Church at Llandudno, which has taken the pews.

(Above) Postcard of St. Paul's Church with the Chetwode Arms across the road. (Left) Newspaper headlines in August 1988.

THE CHRONICLE, WEDNESDAY, APRIL 26, 1989 (Gp 9) **13**

# CHURCH SOLD FOR THE PRICE OF A BEACH HUT

More newspaper reports about the future of St. Paul's. (Above) Reporting the sale for just £20,000 - the same price of a Bournemouth beach hut sold around the same time. (Below) Details about the new venture.

Page 14 - THE GUARDIAN, Friday, May 5, 1989

# Disused church to be centre for community

A DISUSED church in Crewe — one of the town's major landmarks — is set to become a hive of community activities, thanks to the ambitious plans of a local Christian group.

St Paul's Church, Hightown, has been empty for four years, but Crewe Christian Concern are set to transform it into a special community resource centre.

The plans — which will almost certainly be approved by the local council — have the strong backing of the church owners, the Diocese of Chester, and will provide a base for a whole host of local voluntary organisations.

"The aim of the centre is not to duplicate existing services but to fill gaps in provision," said Three C's founder John McCallum, "The building could provide accommodation for local voluntary organisations such as Dial-a-Ride, Relate Marriage Guidance and the toy library group."

Among the facilities already pencilled in:

• a non-alcohol bar — called 'The Prodigals', the bar will have a full cocktail service and regular discos, all alcohol-free.

• computer workshop — where unemployed people can learn the basics of hi-tech language.

• a crèche and snack bar — where mums can come and rest and get the kids off their hands for a while.

There will also be a wide range of adult education facilities, especially aimed at the unemployed.

■ The exciting project is already in motion, although our picture (right) shows just how much work lies ahead!

(Below) 3Cs founder John McCallum (standing left) with two supporters, after taking possesion of the building.

(Above) The canoe makes its appearance. (Below) Eamon and Christine Bundred with some of the first items of furniture.

# People rally to help flood disaster victims

THE people of Crewe have dug deep into their attics to help the flood victims of Towyn refurbish their homes.

Appeals for furniture were made to Chronicle readers after the disaster swamped the inhabitants of the Welsh resort, forcing them out of their houses.

John McCallum, Development Director at the St. Paul's Centre, Hightown, Crewe, is co-ordinating the collection organised by the Salvation Army and Crewe Christian Concern.

He said 'Our first delivery will be made on Thursday. Already we have had a lot of stuff delivered to the centre - in fact we are starting to get chocker!

### Appraisal

'Towyn is well known as an extremely popular holiday and retirement area for many people in this area. There are lots of Crewe people who have friends in the resort.'

John went to Towyn to get an on-the-spot appraisal of the situation.

'All the grass is dead and the ruined furniture is being removed from houses where damaged plaster is being ripped

### By John Leyland

from the walls.

'Very few have been able to move back in and some people will not be able to return to their houses until August.

### Anxious

'However, we have been offered a warehouse for the donated furniture by the local authority.

'There is a definite need for this stuff. People are extremely anxious, especially because there is a high incidence of victims not being insured.

'One of our biggest problems is that we need more vehicles for daytime collections in the Crewe area - although we are getting help from two local companies who will loan works vans to us.

'People are supplying us with lots of stuff - bedding, suites and beds - but we are still desperate for children's items such as prams and cots.'

John McCallum with his church full of furniture bound for Towyn. (M5412P9)

(Opposite page) Richard and Dave (top) with our first proper van. (Centre) St. Paul's as it was when we went in search of a cooker. (Bottom) The early years team getting ready for a Friday sale. (Above) Newspaper report regarding the Towyn flood disaster that started the furniture scheme. (Below) Friday sales always attract a crowd looking for a bargain.

(Above) Myself and Keith examining the new structure for the full mezzanine floor. (Below) Graham with a pile of beds on the first mezzaine floor covering half of the church.

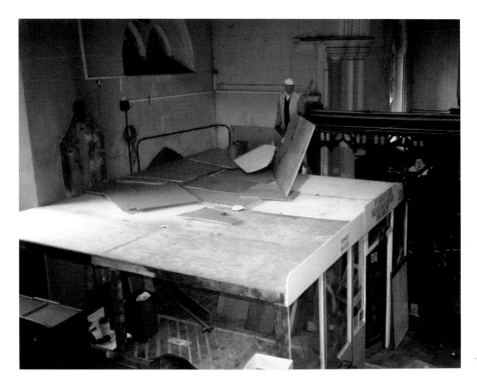

(Above) Donated NatWest desks help to make the first workshop. (Below) The school uniform recycling project was one of many which Cheryl was involved with.

(Above) Hundreds of sheets of sandpaper were used in the workshop to bring life to old furniture. (Below) Article about funding, to employ Derek in the workshop, seen here with Dave. (Opposite page, top) Fun day at Westminster Park with Ben displaying his cycle skills. (Opposite page, bottom) A cycle refurbished in Crewe sent to the Kalene Mission in Zambia.

# Skills scheme will benefit community

**by SUSAN YOUNG**

A FURNITURE restoration scheme has been launched in the West End to give local people extra skills and more choice in what they buy.

The workshop, run by 3C Teamwork at the St Paul's Centre in Hightown, will complement their furniture recycling scheme and the skills can then be passed on to local people.

The West End Project has provided the money, from the Government's Single Regeneration Budget grant, with the aim of establishing the community business in its first year

It should then become self financing through 3C's regular Friday and Saturday furniture sales and the furniture can be sold on to local people.

"Furniture restoration is a very useful addition to our work," said Rob Wykes, 3C Teamwork director.

"3C Teamwork is keen to encourage skills training and this scheme should also benefit the community with a greater choice of items for sale."

*Furniture restoration trainer Derek Wright passes on some skills to student David Curry, left. SANT6258-18.*

(Above) Joan still smiling after 19 years of volunteering, having joined us at the start of the school uniform project. (Below, left) Ray, a real gem of a character, in his favourite place. (Below, right) Steve and Christine both came as volunteers and became staff members.

(Above) Phil and Mel at the sharp end loading furniture to help make a house a home. (Below) Spreading the word and having fun at the Cheshire Show 2016 - Isaac, myself, June and Paul.

(Top) Crewe's first Kosovan refugees arrived at Keele services in the back of a lorry, seen here with Joy.

(Above) Myself and Gordon prepare for an epic journey with aid for Kosovan refugees.

(Above) Kosovan refugees in Albania. The elderly lady was carried over the mountains by her son on her left. (Below) No English was used, but this refugee expressed his thanks by a handshake and touching his heart.

(Above) Isaac - proud of his new found skill and confidence. (Below) Cheryl with Jerry at Thursday computer club. Jerry is celebrating his 60th birthday. (Opposite page) 1. Peter our longest serving chairman. 2. "Rolls- Royce" Robbie. 3. Stephanie our earth rod. 4. Colin the bolt of lightning. 5. Chris who does the work of 10 men. 6. Full shelves in the food bank puts a smile on Audrey's face and full tummies for those who needed it. 7. Geoff, a beautiful person. He made this jigsaw to help him write his name. 8. Peter, the longest serving of St. Paul's Centre users - 27 years and still going strong.

1.

2.

3.

4.

5.

6.

7.

8.

(Above) Explaining what St. Paul's Centre is all about to Prince Edward. (Below, left) Always smiling John. (Below, right) Preperation work by Alexia before a supported adult completes the up-cycling of a mirror.

like a tap running full on, gushing energy, then a small turn and nothing. Our bodies flushed with emotions; disappointment, relief, failure. I instantly began to think about what I would say to people; how I would account for the money we had spent getting to nowhere. Encountering this kind of build-up and deflation is never easy to handle. We were both feeling helpless.

We returned to normal life, whilst over the next 78 days the television reported some 38,000 sorties, with over 10,000 of them missile strikes. The conflict in Kosovo was an expression of humanity at its worst. The world stood by watching as hundreds of thousands of men women and children were displaced, killed and forced to flee once familiar land. The term 'genocide' became commonplace. For the first time since the Second World War, people in Europe feared the growing conflict. The images we saw of stick thin men behind chain link fencing were now, in the present, and not a documentary on the German camps of the 1940s. Something of significance had to be done.

Before I go on to explain how Cheryl and I readied ourselves to fly into the area of conflict, let me share a lesson I learned during this time. As a young man, I had attended some karate classes. Memories of the moves are long gone, yet I was taught one thing that never left me. Standing firm with your core in balance and secure, you launch an attack. During the Kosovan crisis, one word kept coming up time and again: Sortie. This is a French word meaning exit. In military terms this word is much less about the target or enemy than about the position from where an attack is launched. Sortie is about an exit from a defensive position.

Over the weeks and months leading to my subsequent visit to Albania, and ultimately Derje, I recognised that we do our best work in supporting people when we are anchored. My thoughts dwelt on the idea of having a strong platform, a place from which we could reach out. Without complex study or reading psychology books, I realised in 1999 that nothing we set out to achieve would make sense if there was not a solid base in my life, and in that of the charity to launch from. It seemed to me that having significant relationships was fundamental. My faith or relationship to God had to be the central pivot around which everything else would work. This sounds obvious, and many writers have ably explained the principle. However, I came to understand the need for a personal revelation or calling.

Over the years, faith is tested to the limit and there are dark times. A cloud descends, engulfing our private world. Depression does not have to be diagnosed to exist. There is as much brokenness in the church family as there is anywhere else, on occasions even more! Had I known at the start of my life in church ministry that fellow Jesus followers would inflict deep pain in me, I might have not grasped the plough, let alone been tempted to look back. This may be a strange statement, but I learned that I could trust nobody else with the job of sustaining my faith. What if they were weak when I needed them to be strong? As counter intuitive as it sounds, the statement by Paul the Apostle, speaking of God, "My grace is sufficient for you, for My power is made perfect in weakness," sums up the attitude needed to make it through. I did not abandon trust in others, but I elevated trust in God.

Importantly, whilst I was to lead the charity and we had a desire to retain our Christian heritage, my personal faith needed to remain intact. Often it has been fragile, even bordering on brokenness, but my faith has remained intact at the core of my being, held there by the truth that God's grace is indeed sufficient.

If there were to be an order to the bases or foundations from which the charity could launch raids on poverty, or whatever metaphor we might use, the Trustees and key team members also needed to identify with the faith from which Christian Concern derived its life. It seemed to me that our work was motivated, driven and empowered by our belief in God and calling. This brought inevitable conflict.

Winding the clock back a little to September 1998, I was sitting in my office working on a report focused on our support of vulnerable adults. My office and reception were parted by a thin wall of timber beams sectioned to create a frame of windows. These windows were filled at the bottom with 10-millimetre fibre board and glass at the top. So thin was the wall, that on the quietest of days I could hear the water bubbling in the reception fish tank. Being nosy it provided me with a constant distraction.

That day, rounded tones of broken English poured through the wall. The accents were unfamiliar and far too interesting to just let the moment pass. Awkwardly, one of the staff members was attempting to converse. Finding it all too tempting, I interrupted and asked where they were from? "Kosovo," was the answer. In an instant, I realised that there stood before me refugees, in our reception in little old Crewe.

Genti, the vocal one, was the natural leader. We later became friends. Our family watched him and Adelina, his wife, bring Gracie, their daughter, into the world, creating a family. Genti, Adelina, Riza, Enkeleida and a teenage boy had been placed in small apartments near to St. Paul's Centre. Their quest was simple, to find some pillows to make sleep more comfortable. Thirty minutes later, they left amidst handshakes and smiles, with more than just pillows, and a promise to visit them later that day.

Having travelled as a younger man through Greece, Turkey, Iran, Pakistan and India, the depth and sincerity of my new-found friends hospitably came without surprise. Leaving Adelina and Genti's flat that afternoon, full of sweet delights, I decided that St. Paul's Centre must have a role to play in helping the Kosovan people. Their apartment was small in every way. Within two strides you could leave the outside world and be in the kitchen, smaller than that found on a day boat in the local marina. Sitting on the toilet meant knees pressed hard against the door and the bedroom; the living room and kitchen were one. Creatively, an estate agent could make it sound cosy, comfortable, compact and bijou. I sat on one of the two chairs they had whilst Adelina insisted on feeding me. Genti gave me a traditional drink, which meant I couldn't drive home.

"Tell me how you got here?" I asked. "In a lorry to Keele services, on the M6 motorway," Adelina said excitedly. I looked at them both; she was young and pretty but carried the weight of travel about her. He was tough-looking with a wise but cheeky smile. I knew Genti was a survivor. Over the next hour, they told their story. How he had run a café in his home town of Pristina. Men had come with guns. Shots were fired and Genti was hit by a ricochet bullet. Half his thumb was missing. He described how he packed the wound with cheese to stop the bleeding. Cheese! What kind of first aid course had he been on? They fled. Long periods of hiding, walking and sleeping rough passed quickly in the days that followed the shooting up of their home. Over hills, through woodland and on into Albania their tired bodies had carried them. In Albania, they had met up with Riza and Enkeleida. Genti had money and paid the Italian mafia to take them across in a dinghy. He told me how frightened everyone was, then looked me in the eye. "This is the reason that I had a gun," he said. His head nodded slowly as he spoke but his eyes did not leave mine. The money they had paid included safe passage to the UK in a lorry. The journey ended five miles from where we were now sat. Or had it?

Before I left, Genti said with pride that he did not want charity. "Where are all the restaurants and cafés in this town?" he asked. I told him that Nantwich Road in Crewe was a good place to start, and I showed him on a map. The following day he walked to the beginning of that road and knocked on every establishment that sold food. At the end of the road is the town called Nantwich, nearly five miles away. It was there that he got a break. Genti became the salad prep man, five nights a week, in a Turkish restaurant.

We lost touch for a while with Adelina and Genti, but some years later, some friends and I had a meal in an Italian restaurant on the outskirts of our town. It was a delightful place, with a rustic atmosphere and great reputation, the kind of place you go to for a special meal. It was my wife's birthday. We ordered and waited. Moments later the waiter came over and said the head chef would like us to accept two bottles of wine with his compliments. At the end of our meal, the head chef joined us at the table to bring us up to date how he, Adelana and Gracie were getting on. I have never doubted the contribution immigrants make to any nation, especially Britain. They came for pillows and gave us passion for a nation in trouble.

Coincidently, around that same time, a group of local ministers were meeting at St. Paul's Centre for prayer every Friday morning. It was during one of these prayer times that we collectively had a strong sense that it was right for the church in Crewe to respond. In less than four weeks, Gordon Dean and I were driving towards the Port of Dover, and on to Albania.

## ALBANIA CALLING...

Gordon was a delightful man to become acquainted with. We had met on a few occasions and scarcely knew any details of each other's lives. Over the coming weeks, months and years we became good friends, sharing the journey of life and all that it threw at us.

He has a warm, soft face which gives you early warning that his responses will be considered. Gordon is the kind of person whose depth of faith challenges most other Christians. He does not judge or direct when talking to you, but his language is immersed in his sense of hope, healing and hospitality. His belief in miracles was a miracle. I remember he once laid his hand on a washing machine and prayed for it to be fixed in the way you might pray for someone to be healed. It didn't work!

Early on, I learned not to say we needed something too flippantly, as his retort: "Well, have you asked God for it?" was delivered without fail. It was easy to relax with Gordon because he didn't complicate the friendship. He cared for you and gave you time. He was always a great listener, calm with a sense of joy in his life. If we were books, he would be in the 'counselling' section and I would be found under 'extreme sports.' If there was any disconnect in our joint endeavours, it would be that during his pause to pray for the sea to part, I would be building a boat.

Now the pressure was on to get there as soon as possible. Albania was calling. My way of dealing with things is first to decide what we are doing, and then to get on and do it. Many books will tell you about long and structured planning, with risk assessments and asset registers. In the space of a few weeks, we collected food, loaded and fuelled up a van. We were ready, or so we thought.

With our families waving, Gordon and I gingerly set off from St. Paul's Centre. Both of us were conscious of the weight in the van. It wasn't overloaded, honest officer, as we had driven to a friendly local scrap yard and checked it on their weigh bridge. However, it was not under loaded either!

After several hours, battling the UK traffic, we reached the ferry port at Dover in a largely uneventful way - except for one item. Let me mention the briefcase. On the morning of our departure, Gordon insisted on having a briefcase in the cab. I was opposed to this on the grounds of space. "I will keep it on my side of the cab," he promised, and proceeded to hold it as though it contained gold bullion. I looked at him, an eyebrow raised, but appreciated that he was very touchy about that case.

Soon after we had gotten underway, Gordon pulled the case onto his knees and rested his arms on the lid. I found this distracting and began to wonder what it contained. For the briefest moment, I wondered if I was sharing the trip with a dangerous and escaped mental health patient. Just past Stafford services he casually clicked open the briefcase clasps, one on each side. He raised the lid no more than four inches, and then fiddled around inside the case. First, there was the sound of paper peeling and ripping, followed by a clear snap, or break. His fingers appeared with a tiny piece of chocolate. It was almost microscopic, no more than a slither of chocolate.

"Are you sharing that, or what?" I asked. Somehow, Gordon convinced me he only had enough to last the trip, and that he needed it. He admitted to having a problem with chocolate, so I left it at that. In my mind, I had an image of this small bar of chocolate being consumed no more than one lick an hour, across two weeks! However, I knew he had more; the case was full, a mobile Type 2 diabetes factory. I decided to leave him to it.

As I stood, looking out to sea with the UK growing smaller, an immense sense of adventure and foreboding came over me. No sooner had the sight of England's white cliffs disappeared, the horizon delivered France to us. My gaze lingered on the passing sea, watching the sharpness of the ship's bow cut a route through the vastness of the channel. Would

I return, would I see my home again? These questions raced through my mind – and the gut of my stomach. I always hated being away from Cheryl; loneliness finds such an easy foothold within me. Thankfully, the foaming water and the bow metres below were so mesmerising they helped the time pass.

Truth-be-told, I had not given our 'mission' a lot of thought. The risks were obvious and included the possibility of getting shot. The assets were a van, some food and two unknown blokes from a town virtually unheard of – Crewe. Saying "I am going" had seemed to be the right thing to say at the prayer meeting. Filling boxes and talking to the newspaper had a momentum about it, which easily drowned out any doubts or questions. We were heading for a dangerous place where anything could happen. Indeed, I did return some weeks later with a scar that took months to disappear.

On French soil, as we left the ferry, we were met by the European challenge. Politics or culture did not feature in this problem. The French people's love of garlic or onions was negotiable. Indeed, the difference in language could be overcome. The problem that hit us, at the noisy metal grid as we left the ferry, was which side to drive on! This was not my first driving experience in France, but the first in a small commercial vehicle. Remember, we did not have Satnav in those days. The maps were large scale, not much more than a flattened globe. I was making it up as I went along.

Our extensive travel plan was as follows: France - tunnel to Italy - go south in Italy to a port - ferry to Albania - then ask for Steven Martin in Tirana. Mad dogs and Englishmen going out in the midday sun, came to mind. We mastered driving on what I still perceive to be the wrong side of the road and made it a fair way through central France. There is a vastness about the country that begs you to stay and look around as the miles, no, kilometres, pass by. Well, this was not a holiday, it was a mission. Our pleasure or comfort was of no consequence to the journey's purpose.

Bedding down for the night in southern France, Gordon climbed into the back of the van, with his briefcase of course, and made himself a comfortable space amongst the food and clothes. I resisted this because of my childhood fear of enclosed spaces. Of course, I didn't confess this to Gordon. I suggested that I would be more comfortable in the front.

Confession, I should add, does become a feature when you share long days and nights with someone. Gordon and I could share our hopes, fears, disappointments and frustrations. Over the two weeks I spent in close contact with Gordon, I discovered much about myself. In many ways, our trip was a cathartic counselling session. Since neither of us was overly interested in a pity party, it meant we were honest and reflective. Gordon always had a Bible verse to counter my "But I just feel" comments, and I always had a story to illustrate my thought. He did not carry the same insecurities as I, or at least did not show them. "Good night," I said, as I pulled the roller shutter down on Gordon's bedroom for the night.

My resting place was the driver and passenger seats in the cab. The gear stick was problematic. My laid-out body could not fully extend across the seats. No matter which way I turned or curled, it was impossible to find a natural position. My mind was tired but still engaged like a runaway car filled with kangaroo juice, as my dad called it. The night was long, cold and noisy. I woke twice believing I could smell petrol and my imagination had the van soaked in fuel by an anti-something group about to burn us to death. The seats were bench-style for two people, with the driver's seat separated by a space for the handbrake and gear stick. All night I had the sensation of falling through a cavern, which was six inches, perhaps fifteen centimetres, at best. I woke in the morning with my forehead impaled on the round window winder. Looking in the mirror, I could see a perfect circle indented in the centre of my forehead. With colour, it may have given the appearance of conversion to Hinduism. Gordon, on the other hand, needed waking from his comfortable, deep and peaceful sleep.

We travelled on, feasting on the delights of southern France as we approached Italy and the Fréjus tunnel. The snow-capped mountains and dark green forests were stunning, a welcome distraction for us. On the approach to the tunnel, we travelled over a gorge. Nearing the centre of the bridge a gust of wind caught our high-sided van and forced us across a couple of lanes. There were no other vehicles near us, but we both felt a little sick and fragile. I realised at that moment that the threat from one of the three million Kalashnikov rifles knocking around in Albania was not the only risk on this trip. I thought of all those people who had said we were brave to travel to a conflict zone. The truth is, crossing the street or driving a van on an open road could be your last trip.

Entering the tunnel, we were struck by the contrast from picture-perfect postcard Alps to the little red tail lights of the vehicle in front. For eight miles, I concentrated on the lights, tunnel and our speed. We passed a sign that welcomed us to Italy, but the darkness did not abate - although the signs and road markings changed.

The journey through Italy was uneventful and we arrived at the port of Bari just hours before a ship was leaving. We could not have timed it better, except we didn't time it. Our flimsy plan just fell into place. I walked into the town and found some large bottles of water and a pay phone. I spoke with Cheryl. Our conversation was awkward as we were missing each other, and Cheryl was not entirely happy about me going on the trip. This was another adventure I had not properly discussed with her. It would be nice to explain how we prayed and fasted over the opportunity, that we had met with our accountability group and church minister. There are those who would overstate the sense of God's calling which burned in their soul. My confession is that people in Albania were hungry and the compassion of God within me drove my actions. Paul the Apostle used the term 'the love of Christ constrains us to…' and Cheryl was gracious and trusting and, most importantly, did not say what her heart wanted her lips to breathe. She did not say "Come home" during that awkward call.

Gordon and I had to fill out paperwork and buy a ticket for the ferry. We encountered some interesting Italian bureaucratic processes with the port authorities. Like all such government systems, and the people involved, they loved paper - preferably with official stamps on. Anticipating this we had several documents, and copies of these documents, including an inventory of the vehicle's contents. Frustratingly, we had to make several visits to the same office. The officials were in dispute over which paper should be signed, and by whom. It was on the final visit to the port export office that I realised they had assumed we were taking goods from Italy to Albania. Once it became clear that the goods originated in the UK, and were not items for sale, it was smiles all round. In the stroke of a pen, following a tweak in their understanding, we were transformed from dodgy importers to heroes.

The ferry finally lowered its enormous metal door. Bangs, clangs and a loud screeching came from the gigantic mechanism responsible for the process. Lorry after lorry drove up the ramp. Powerful diesel engines revved as the over-laden vehicles hit the ramp, or were shunted into tight corners. We were amongst the last to be loaded. I sat anxiously waiting for the controller's wave. Our little van was like a toy in the belly of the ship dwarfed by everything around it. The ramp was designed for vehicles of up to forty tonnes; ours being just three. Like a complete first-time driver, I took the ramp awkwardly and misguidedly along a channel. The chap directing us on went red and shouted as though I had killed his best friend. Sheepishly, I parked up and walked towards him expecting a barrage of abuse. "You English, you kill me," he said through a beaming smile. His arm rose and grasped my shoulder embracing me. Now I understood what the Mediterranean temperament means – I sound like I'm going to kill you, but I'm going to love you instead.

Arrival in Albania, during such challenging times, was never going to be smooth. Our encounter with the Italian port authority was a warm-up, or so I thought. We drove off the ship and joined a long, snaking line of commercial vehicles; some looked like they had been there a while. They had. The port of Durres was an experience. To our advantage, we had been given a contact beforehand and were expecting to meet a man called Yevgeni at the port. My immediate thought was how anyone could meet us before we passed customs? The guards looked menacing and the whole situation felt hostile. Gordon took it all in his stride, as usual trusting that God would provide a way.

When we made initial contact with the immigration office, we were waved away to wait our turn. Communication was almost non-existent, with no sense of direction or timescale given. Talking to some of the other drivers we discovered many had been waiting days, not hours, to get into Albania. The Kosovan crisis had doubled the traffic flow through Durres. The atmosphere in the port was strange, tense, somehow hanging like over-ripe grapes on a vine waiting to drop. Border guards were poorly paid, poorly equipped and poorly motivated. In short, they were poor. For these men, bribes were not corruption, they were how their families ate in the absence of regular salaries. Bribes or baksheesh were what the 'wait–in–line' was all about.

We sat in the van for a while and wondered what to do. We prayed. We ate. We talked. Gordon announced he needed a pee. Following a brief search, we discovered the facilities were currently not accessible. Gordon said he would go behind the van, while I sat in the driver's seat. The second he disappeared the vehicles in front started to move. So, I pulled the van forward about ten metres. Gordon was suddenly exposed. In the laughter that followed, we both recognised that when you gotta go, you gotta go. Life's essential needs stop for no man, even during chaos.

BANG, BANG, BANG! The repeated thumping on the side of the van startled us both. We jumped up. Staring through the passenger door window was the face of Yevgeni. "Rob, are you Rob?" he asked. The grip of his hand was strong, and the subsequent shake rattled my whole shoulder. He spoke with a low voice, the way all good Russian KGB agents do in the movies. It was hard to catch every word except the last one of each sentence.

"You know what I mean?" was his closer, always long and drawn out. Whatever he said sounded important and he gently worked his neck so his head bobbed in time to the words, ending with a slow drop and poignant pause for those last five words. Yevgeni looked like one of my post-war teachers. He wore a tweed jacket, and he had wavy hair which was not too short, not too long. An unruly tie hung loosely around his neck. His Mediterranean tanned skin, brown eyes and round face made him look Greek. The face of this man appeared like the centre of a railway town - lines everywhere. Yevgeni had a story to tell and it either began or ended with the name Enver Hoxha.

"One of you stay with the van, the other come with me to the import-export office," Yevgeni told us, very matter of fact. Gordon stayed guard whilst I walked with Yevgeni. In my mind, we were going to the office within the compound to show passports and file papers. After all this was the port, the place of entry into the country. We walked past some guards, along a chain-link fence and through a gap. Yes, a gap where the fencing had been carefully cut and peeled back. A blue Ford was waiting for us. We drove into the city of Durres to what looked like a bombed-out building. Everything appeared old and tired, as I must have at this point. My last shower had been days, not hours earlier. More dust rose with every corner the car turned.

Inside the building, we all shook hands expressing excitement to see each other – although I had no idea who they were. Sasha - short, bald and wearing a yellowing suit - was our import sponsor. He owned an import-export business and was a friend of the church. I'm not sure what that meant back then, or even now. I do know that without his help we would have been on the quayside for weeks, or on the next boat back to Italy. Sasha wanted to know all about us. Explaining where Crewe was proved too difficult, so I invoked our tenuous proximity to Manchester United, as it was 30 miles up the road. He commented on how detailed my paperwork was and how helpful it was to have each box in the vehicle labelled. As time passed, I became anxious about Gordon. There was also the feeling of unease about being in the country illegally. No one had seen my passport. I had entered the country via a gap in the border fence.

Returning to the main Durres port area, we re-entered through the secret gap that was seemingly known to all. With Yevgeni by my side, I presented the paperwork to the immigration office. They argued. I watched. They shouted. I watched. They shook hands, so did I. One of the border guards walked us to the van and inspected the contents. Pointing at his feet, he said: "Me, size 9, yes?" I couldn't believe his cheek. "No way," I shouted back and slammed the roller-shutter down. He tried again, and asked for a pair of shoes. Yevgeni wasn't impressed and started waving his arms. The poor guard gave in and sealed the vehicle shutter with a special tag. I have always wondered if he gave in easily because Yevgeni had already oiled the process in the immigration office. Moments later we were heading towards Tirana where the vehicle had to be placed in a compound overnight - for a second import inspection, official or otherwise. It was dark and the roads were isolated. Yevgeni was joined by another man, called Joseph. He was tall and athletic, bright, bouncy, and talked with his whole body engaged when he spoke. He said: "Follow closely behind me and stop for nothing, there are bandits on this road. Do not get out of the vehicle." Gordon chuckled; he did that when danger seemed near.

I'm not sure if there is an entry in the *Guinness Book of Records* for the most potholes on one road, but I know where the winning entry would be. Driving felt more like a fairground ride on the bucking bronco. Staying focused, close-up on the road, took my eyes from the car in front. Joseph had been waved through a road block, and we were directed to the side of the road. Gordon later described those who pulled us over like a group retired from Idi Amin's private guard!

The barrel of a Kalashnikov tapped on my window. I wound it down, slowly, and was ordered to step out of the van. There was an immediate loneliness about this encounter for me. Gordon went straight to prayer and found an inner peace; I dearly wish I could say the same. Internally, deep in my soul, there was an inner peace, but, in my brain, there was a riot of fear and foreboding. They had little English; we had no Albanian. They had guns; we had none. Thankfully, Joseph appeared with Yevgeni and we relaxed. They all shouted at each other; it seemed the way things happened. Joseph walked to one side with a man who was obviously the leader. They patted and shook hands, and our journey continued. In these situations, handshakes are a point of exchange.

Once, as the Railway Mission chaplain, I conducted the funeral of an old engine driver. The place was packed. As the mourners left the Crematorium, one aged gentlemen pressed into my hand a five-pound note, held it there, and said: "Lovely service, Vicar." Was that a bribe, or acknowledgment and appreciation of my work? I learned in Albania that some Christians refused to give even a dollar to oil the works, while others recognised that the officials before them were often not paid for months but still turned up to work. My understanding is that less than fifty dollars to say 'Thank You,' or used as bribes if you'd prefer, helped us get three tonnes of food into hungry bellies.

Walking away from the compound we looked back at the van and Yevgeni asked: "Did those wheels cost much?" I thought it was a strange question. "Why?" I enquired. "Wheels often go missing from this compound overnight," he explained. My stomach felt empty as I glanced back and thought that was probably the last we would see of the van.

Yevgeni took us to meet Steven Martin, our main contact in the country. He was British by birth, lived in New Zealand for most of his life, before becoming a missionary in Albania. Steven seemed to shout at every driver he encountered; he might have known something we didn't. He was impatient with everyone around him, and for a moment I questioned whether to challenge him about it. Eleven years had passed since he had first put foot in the Albanian capital, Tirana. This was a man on the edge, wound so tightly there was a disturbing tension about him. Had I not bothered to listen to him, and soak up his story, I might easily have judged him un-Christian in attitude. Standing before me was a man who had poured his heart into a broken nation, with its broken people and broken infrastructure. Nothing worked. Achieving anything was frustrating. Steven needed a break. The beauty of his faith, his compassion and drive had been on high-alert for years. Underneath this tense exterior, lay a pioneering, creative, good old-fashioned missionary. He left behind a good life in a safe, ordered nation to share his faith in one of the poorest and most broken societies in Europe.

Having driven more than 1,500 miles in three and half days, stealing restless moments of sleep and washing in public toilets, we were ready for the hotel. I looked forward to a long, warm shower and a soft mattress. The idea of drifting off to a sleep, absent of moving vehicles, surrounded by bricks and not thin metal, appealed very much. Tonight, I would lock my hotel door and rest.

Unfortunately, things didn't work out quite the way we had hoped. Ismet, our host, was not a hotelier. He and his wife, Viola, were a delightful couple, friends of the church who saw stabling foreign visitors as encountering God. How disappointing to meet me! Neither of them spoke English, but the ancient language of pointing and smiling worked a treat. A rub of the stomach linked to a chewing motion landed a walk to a pizza shop. As we moved in the dark, tough streets that looked and felt dangerous, Ismet kept us close. Everyone knew him. No shop could be passed without a handshake or back slap. We accompanied a local celebrity, a respected man.

BRRRR, BRRRR! There was rapid gunfire. Gordon was unmoved as he looked around. I ducked and scanned the horizon. Ismet laughed. For him the sound of gunfire was normal. It brought no rise in concern or change of plan. Somehow, he managed to convince us that this was all normal behaviour. We refocused on the food. It was worth the wait. The pizza was warm and tasty, just the filling meal we had craved.

Back at Ismet's house, Gordon and I slept in the living room on couches that resembled a camel's back. Before bedding down, we washed in a half-constructed bathroom with cold water. Ismet insisted on giving us a nightcap. The shock of this liquid running down my throat burned like fire, then ran into a warm, itchy feeling to my inner ear. Then I slept.

Seven hours later, my mind slowly woke to the new day. I had no memory of the night, so I assumed that I had slept well. We were both rested and ready for what the day might deliver. The house in which we sat was fortress like. There were few windows looking out, and those that did revealed high walls or fencing. Ismet was building their house from reclaimed materials. He was proud of his work but had no sense of rush towards completion. There was a typical look about most of the houses; half started, half finished. It was hard to tell if they were going up or coming down – everywhere was a building site, or bomb site, with subtle differences.

Breakfast was strange: smelly cheese and bread. We ate with gratitude following prayer. "Please Lord, help me look as though I'm enjoying this and please, whatever happens, keep it down – Amen." This was to become a standard cry at meal times.

Our guide Edmundo arrived to take us to the International Baptist Centre, our ultimate destination. Before leaving, and speaking through Edmundo, we thanked Ismet and Viola. We explained how safe we felt with them. At this he smiled, and then busily moved us back into the house. Lifting the lid of the sofa on which Gordon had slept, Ismet withdrew a Kalashnikov. So, we had slept with an illegal firearm in the room, an AK-47 that had, apparently, seen action. Ismet had military experience in his background and handled the weapon with ease of movement. Gordon and I posed with the gun, surprised at its feel, even comfort of design. We were assured it was a weapon of defence and of the last resort.

Judging Ismet was not an option. Living in a civil western democracy with a police force that didn't carry guns had made it easy for me to distrust, dislike even, such weapons. Living in rural Cheshire, where the woods are for pleasure, not hiding, and we call the police because the neighbours play their music too loud, had somewhat insulated me from Ismet's experience of life.

Everyone in Albania knew someone who had been shot. You could not say that in Britain. Leaving Ismet and Viola, we drove to the church and then to the food distribution centre. Our work was about to begin.

## REAL, HUNGRY PEOPLE

My heart sank as the sight of so many people greeted us at the collection point. Stories of sorrow and pain were written all over their faces. Not a single overweight person in sight. I wanted them to look well-fed and smiling, but they didn't. Things had suddenly got very real.

"You'll have to be firm or they will over-run us," said Steven, as we stepped down from the vehicle. The collection point was a brick building with large metal doors on rusty runners. The opening was wide enough for our van but there was no space to park it inside, because the plan was to empty half of the aid here and then move on.

Lifting the van's shutter, we were surrounded by men. They held on tightly to their dignity, restraining the natural urge to grab the food they needed. They wanted to give help, and they wanted to receive help. Together, we unloaded the boxes and placed them inside the building. Forming a small production line, we put stuff into a bag and passed it along. My job was to put in one bag of flour and one of sugar, then pass to the next man in the line, who added tomatoes and rice.

With my task done, I joined the team up front giving out the bags. An efficient and stern-voiced man sat with a list of names. As each person presented themselves, all men, he said: "Emri lutem," translated as "Name, please?"

"Pavli," came the first reply. Then "Si anëtarë të familjes njeri me ty?" was, I later discovered, a question about the number of family members. I felt uncomfortable about this process of questioning – after all, they were hungry and broken, I thought.

"I have two daughters, six and eight years old, and my wife, who is sick," was Pavli's reply to the probing and, in my opinion, intrusive line of questioning. A tick was placed beside his name and he moved along to me. I looked him in the face and smiled. It was pathetic; I did not know what to say. I thought of my two daughters and wife, who were not sick. They were all warm, safe and well. Pavli was a bloke just like me, except his world had been ripped from beneath his feet. He smiled and walked away towards his precious family. The girls looked lost, and without the energy to be excited or inquisitive about the contents of the bag their father had just received. They were not on holiday in a foreign country, picking up a treat before spending the day at the beach. I wanted to know more, to do more.

Before I could drift further into daydreams, wondering what else I could do to help, there was a scuffle. A man lost his place in the queue and tried to re-enter. Patience was wearing thin and the tension was rising. Steven moved as quickly as the sound travelled. He shouted, and he was good at that. It looked wrong and inappropriate, but it worked and peace was restored. Later, he explained how dithering usually ended in tears and that the situation needed a quick closure.

Soon after, I announced: "No more food parcels today" and helped to lock up the building. Everyone had received something, but it did not feel enough. Then something bizarre happened. We were prevented from entering the van by the refugees. They insisted on thanking us, shaking hands with everyone. A tall, thin man, wearing a green tartan waistcoat (donated, I'm sure) held my right hand with his. I didn't catch his name, just the expression on his olive-skinned face sat beneath a mop of grey hair. He stroked his chest over his heart whilst looking me in the eye, so captivating I could not look away. In a moment of pure, naked humanity he moved his left hand from over his heart and placed it on mine. "Thank you," he said.

Returning the following morning, our task was to visit people the church were working more closely with, programmes to prepare them for a possible return after the troubles. A lady called Jenny and several students joined us in preparing the parcels which could now be more specific. We had the ages of the children in the family, and details of their general needs. I was struck by the way these people worked tirelessly, serving in a context they had not set out to do. Many of them were young Bible college students taking some time out to work in a cross-cultural setting. When they had agreed to come out to Albania, neighbouring Kosovo was not at war, nor had Albania's population almost doubled. These were resilient and responsive people doing what needed to be done.

The first home we entered was full. Culturally, it was impossible for us to walk in and walk out again. We had to stay, to eat or drink. The very thought of eating the aid we had brought troubled me. "Please take it," said the man, as he handed me a glass of Coke. I can't stand Coke, but this was not the moment to declare it. He had made a gesture. I was grateful.

The room was square with a rug in the centre upon which sat a low table. It had thin, spindly legs and small mosaic tiles on top. The whole atmosphere felt Arabic. The women were in the background, the men sat proud and dignified. Besnik wore a polo shirt and jacket. His receding hair line and moustache elongated his head. His rounded shoulders and slight lean forward made him look like he was carrying something. He was the head of the family, and anxious to ensure we were comfortable and blessed. We exchanged pleasantries, then I asked the question, a stupid question, the same question I had asked of Genti months earlier in Crewe. "Tell me, how did you get here?" I asked once again.

Through broken English, and some careful interpretations by the translator, he told his story. "We were in a small village where we grew up. My brothers and I worked on our farm which has been in the family for three generations. The soldiers came and told us that we would have to leave. We knew they were killing Kosovans without reason. After many anxious days and the sight of our neighbour's farm burning, we all agreed to leave."

I asked if they knew where they would go, and if it would be better. He continued: "My younger brother was killed in the first weeks of the war. My older brother and I cared for his widow and three children. We were eleven in the group, including our mother. The soldiers came banging at the door and shouting. They ordered us to leave, calling us dogs. In our rush to get out, my mother had to be carried."

For a short moment, I struggled to take in what he had said. So, I asked him more. "How far did you carry your mother?" His response sounded unbelievable, fantasy beyond imagination. The room was quiet and mother was sat in a chair whilst Besnik sat beside her, on the arm, as though they were joined. "I carried her to the edge of our village and rested. Nearby, I found an old wooden wheelbarrow from a neighbour's farm. I used this for a few miles until we came close to the centre of the forest below the hills. We slept. The following morning everyone helped to put mother on my back and I carried her. We travelled a little in the day but hid mostly and travelled greater distances at night. Always I walked with mother on my back. It was hard. We covered less than 30 kilometres some days, but after two weeks we crossed into Albania."

His rounded shoulders, and that lean forward, were no longer a mystery to me. We were sitting in a room with a man who loved his mother. The translator whispered in my ear: "She's ninety." In that moment, I knew the journey for her must have been excruciating, yet she sat straight-backed, head held high, unfazed by the fuss of these strange foreigners bearing gifts. While we sat, some of the children had gone through the boxes we brought. They were trying on clothes, garments donated by children like them but living in Crewe where bad people didn't burn your house because of your ancestry.

During the day, we went from one home to another, hearing stories that hours of counselling neither would nor should dislodge. Our lives were touched and changed. One lady, in her mid-fifties, with two teenage children, a boy and a girl, told of her husband being taken into the garden and shot. How do you recover from that, and where do you start? She was investing all she could muster into her children, speaking of education and degrees. Her sights were set on the future, and we came away with a sense that she was rising above the hatred and the downward spiral of self-destruction all around her.

On the last visit of our day, we met a young family. There was a man and wife, with two boys, four and eight. They shared a single room with a curtain divider. On the other side was the man's sister-in-law with her four-year-old twins, a girl and boy. She was a widow of the conflict, but too fragile to share the story. There was no need to ask. For me, it was clear that the black male blazer she wore with chrome buttons was her husband's. This was her sense of his presence. Her brother-in-law now had two families to support and protect. I wondered if he had yet found the emotional space to grieve his brother.

St. Paul's Centre, Crewe, could do in Albania for Kosovans what it does for the locals – extend a practical hand in a time of need. Kosovo was an immense global tragedy. Known as the Balkan conflict, in which the word genocide became familiar once again throughout Europe, we played our part. Ours was a small part that will not feature in the grand scheme of events, nor land in a record of historical account. Unworthy of knighthood notoriety, and yet to a handful of people our part gave rise to hope and restored a measure of lost dignity.

There is a passage in the Bible that leaves some of us cold. Jesus is reported as saying this: "I was hungry and you didn't feed me, I was thirsty and you did not give me a drink." This, of course, was followed, from the righteous around him, with the retort: "When were you hungry and thirsty?" You can almost see them with a startled look, shaking heads in that disbelieving way, as Jesus points out that anyone with hunger or thirst was He.

Jesus wasn't about the business of generating mass guilt in us or suggesting we attempt to solve every problem we encounter. Put quite simply – we can't, but the challenge is to do what we can. The community at St. Paul's Centre did what it could, and I had the privilege of being the final hand that gave the cup of water to a thirsty person in God's name.

## BEAUTIFUL SOULS

During my first days at St. Paul's Centre, I often discovered new people and activities as I explored the building. One day, I walked through the dark-oak double doors into the church. I had done that several times, but the sight that greeted me always filled me with wonder. On the right was the font; one of the biggest I have ever seen. It was carved from granite, with a wooden lid formed like a cartwheel, with a cast iron handle. The vicars of St. Paul's must have had arms like Popeye! Near the font, and filling the corner of the church, stood a work bench, tool cupboards and strips of wooden off-cuts stacked in the shape of a tepee.

Everything was covered in dust, made more visible by the stream of sunlight that poured in to light up the whole space around the font. The sun's angle, warmth and haze were perfect, almost creating a Midsomer Murder crime scene. That morning, to the right of this scene, was the silhouetted figure of an oddly-shaped man. There was no reason to be alarmed, but I was intrigued by who he was. I held out my hand and walked towards him. "Hello!" I said. His eyes met mine and I felt my soul awaken. "Aw-right," was his response, spoken in a low and gravelly voice.

Wearing a green overcoat, listing to one side and sporting a curly perm, this mysterious figure cut an odd shape. He was hunched over a chair, which was positioned sideways against a bench. The chair was half brown, half pine coloured, with a straight line of separation, at the end of which was the man's hand. He was holding a piece of sandpaper, worn and frayed at the edges, and yet his grip on it was vice-like as though it were a bar of gold.

A voice from behind me broke the silence. "That's all Raymond can do," shouted out a man, walking with purpose past where I was standing. I looked back at the eyes in the corner, and said: "So you're Raymond. Well, I'm Rob…" He smiled back, and drew me towards him. "This is my work; it's a chair, and what you do is rub the paint off, see!"

He was so proud of his work, enthusiastic and clearly thinking that I needed to hear the details. I was fascinated, but it took me a while to tune into his voice. Many years of fits and falls from epilepsy had taken their toll on Raymond. His speech was not clear, and his words were ill-formed. After a few minutes, it was time for me to walk on. I reached out with my left hand and placed it on his bony shoulder, looked him in the face, and said: "You're a good man, Raymond, well done." He smiled back, and said: "Thanks, boss."

For the next 15 years, I saw Raymond at some point most weeks. Many Christmases he also came to our home as a member of the family. He became my friend, and I became his boss.

"That's all Raymond can do," was heard too often. That comment, condemning Raymond to a limited experience of life was for me, as the saying goes, like a red rag to a bull. I discovered through exploring this comment that the views held by some of the volunteers and staff needed to be challenged. Raymond was an adult with learning difficulties, a term which makes most of us uncomfortable because the range of people this description covers is vast.

Around the centre, and across society in general, people tend to see those with learning difficulties as other, and identified them more by what they could not do than what they could. Can you imagine going through life described by your inadequacies or limits?

"Greetings, can I introduce you to my friend Rob, he can't fly because he's too fat," is how some might see me. I wanted to prove that Raymond could do more, and at the same time show that he did not need to do more simply to become one of us, or become an equal part of the team to make everyone feel more comfortable about themselves. I decided that, over subsequent months, Raymond was going to change the shape of the charity and help place some flesh on the bones of the vision.

In recent years, the terminology used to describe people with differing levels of capacity has been a moving feast of verbs and nouns. To name but a few: adults with learning difficulties, adults with additional needs, adults with special needs and, latterly, vulnerable adults. We all understand the challenge; none of us want to be condescending, yet at the same time we want to be clear if there are special needs to be considered.

An academic named Henri Nouwen once lived in a community of people with disabilities. His experience taught him a precious lesson about his own place in the world. Henri discovered, by living in a community with vulnerable adults, that their like or dislike of him would not be based on their knowledge of the many books he had written, as they had not read them. He discovered that he was simply one of the group, and whilst he could find reasons to be set apart, they could not. They were defined as different merely by name, as opposed to achievement or notoriety.

Our battle, it seemed to me, was to correctly define those amongst us as part of us, regardless of ability. We needed to learn to journey together and focus not on differences but shared experience. What was special about Raymond could be said about any of us. Over the years, I heard Raymond, and most of the people now termed vulnerable adults, use the expression 'we' more than 'I' when speaking about their place within the centre. This is key to understanding what is special about St. Paul's Centre: that we are a community is more important than our individuality. Two female social workers visited one day, and I showed them around the centre. Following a drink of tea, and general chat, I took them into our main office and began introducing them to the team. Raymond stood at the back of the office just watching. He often came in and waited for someone to ask what he wanted. He stood and stared without making comment.

That morning, as we drew closer to him, without a prompt, Raymond asked one of the social workers a question. To this day, I have no idea what was in his mind at the time. His question may not have been what he really wanted to know. Raymond spoke in a low tone, from the back of his throat, and when his words were clear there was the air of a gangster about his voice.

Raymond looked directly at the social worker in the pretty blue summery dress, and said: "What colour knickers you got on?" She did not blink, and before she could respond, I said: "Oh, do you need some more sandpaper, Raymond?" I then led the ladies out of the office and continued the tour. His question did not offend or shock, nor did it require a response.

In the time that has passed since then, we have journeyed with many who were working through brain injuries. Their language, on occasions, was foul and we needed to accept it as a symptom of the injury, not a statement of their heart.

One man at St. Paul's Centre, called Andrew, even taught himself to prefix all sentences with "I'm sorry, I have a brain injury," when he spoke. If he didn't get that in first, he ended with "I'm sorry, I have a brain injury," before anyone could reply. This became helpful on occasions, because his comments were uncensored adolescent thoughts. He once asked my wife why she bothered with me, and asked her to kiss him and try the goods. She didn't.

I can always remember the joy of hearing him cursing loudly. Following his accident, he spent over a year in a coma, then ten years in a wheelchair and two more on crutches. That morning, when I heard him curse, it was because he had progressed to using one walking stick, soon discarding it having walked the length of the centre without it. For ten minutes, he forgot about his disability and walked normally. How beautiful it was hearing "I've lost my ******* walking stick!" to those who knew the significance of the profanity.

Over the years, we have learned to just accept certain behaviour from those we work with. It is, in some ways, important not to be shocked or disappointed. Particularly in the early days, things happened that we can now smile about, but at the time they challenged us.

Soon after my first encounter with Raymond, and through the inspiration of another wonderful man, Dave, we had a real workshop area to work in. Along the journey towards creating this workshop, I tried to change the behaviour and outlook of the volunteers and staff. My aim was to re-educate them so that they viewed Raymond and the other vulnerable adults as part of the team. This has never been fully successful, because with the arrival of every new volunteer or staff member the challenge to educate is revisited. The ethos and values are rooted in documents and held in the hearts of most of the team, but never 100% and never all the time. Through this we learned it is an ongoing journey, and that we will never arrive at a place of completion.

Knowing how a person arrived at a given place helps to understand them more, to appreciate the nuances of their behaviour. Raymond had been in an institution, Cranage Hall, for a long period of his life. At the height of its use, Cranage Hall had 520 beds for male and female patients, and was originally run by the Cheshire Joint Board for the Mentally Defective. During Raymond's time there, the beds reduced and the activities increased.

There are many stories of a hard existence at Cranage Hall, but Raymond never said a negative word about it. In the late eighties, it was closed and the patients mostly returned to their home towns. Raymond, along with others who worked with us, returned to the Crewe area. Raymond went to live with the Lady Verdin Trust.

St. Paul's Centre became a new way of living for Raymond. At Cranage Hall, everything was on site and the routine was regimented; he was not an individual. That said, it became clear that Raymond was a survivor and cared for others.

Some years after he joined us, we had another encounter with a social worker visiting St. Paul's Centre. This is not, I hasten to say, another story about knickers! As I walked into the workshop with the social worker, I noticed a slight hesitation on her part. We spoke with Raymond, Geoff, Alex and the trainer that day. They each showed their work, planters, a foot stool, and Raymond was making a bird box.

Walking back towards the office I noticed the lady was tearful, so I paused. "Is everything okay?" I asked. "Was that Raymond Shenton in the workshop, the Raymond that was once in Cranage Hall?" she questioned. "Yes, he's been here for a few years now, do you know him?"

At that moment, I was invited to explore part of Raymond's character and history I had not known before. She began to describe an incident that took place when she worked at Cranage Hall. She was pregnant at the time, and a patient had lost control and was becoming violent with her. She felt vulnerable and frightened, isolated from the other staff. "

Without warning or prompt, Raymond appeared, tackled the other patient and rescued me," she revealed. Holding a handkerchief to her moist eyes, she added: "Without him stepping in, I don't know what would have become of me or my baby."

On many assessment forms, and in medical records, Raymond is described as a vulnerable adult. Yet, on that day in question, he switched roles with a caring professional who wore the robe of vulnerability and required another to care. Those that knew Raymond have stories of his cantankerous behaviour. "Stubborn to the core," was how one of the team would often describe him. I wonder whether we could all be described like that at times, multi-faceted, capable of doing good on Monday and harm on Tuesday? Raymond's stubbornness was independence to him; his acts of kindness were a recognition of what is right in civil society.

Building a workshop brought a new life to St. Paul's Centre. That space enthused us and instilled creativity. We have had three of them over the years, each one being an improvement of the previous. From the first room made from NatWest Bank's old desks, to the last that was designed and built with bought materials, they all provided an area for creativity. Raymond would take a keen interest in the sale of anything he made or refurbished. He moved on from sandpaper to drills, planes and even a bandsaw. Whenever I showed people around and he talked about something he was working on, we would look at each other as he finished. "And that's not all he can do," I would say with great delight.

As a community, it was our privilege to know Raymond until his last days. He became ill and slowly drifted away from this world. He had such a strong presence of mind and keen understanding of what was going on around him. When the doctor told him that he had cancer, Raymond declined treatment and made it clear he would not die in hospital. Within weeks we sat on the edge of his bed, saying goodbye.

On Wednesday November 2, 2011, St. Paul's Centre closed for the day and we joined scores of Raymond's friends to celebrate his life. We concluded that we had been the beneficiaries of an encounter with a most extraordinary man.

It didn't stop with Raymond. "Be alright in a bit," was Geoff's phrase that rang out through the centre for many years, coming from the mouth of a man more giving than most. He, like Raymond, was also a former Cranage Hall patient. Profoundly deaf, he wore hearing aids, but not well. For the first few years of knowing him, he could be heard coming by the buzzing sound of the hearing aid switched to the wrong setting.

Geoff's delightfully infectious grin was such that by distorting his face he brought the centre to a standstill on many occasions. His sense of humour and timing was faultless. As a child, he never attended school, instead staying at home on a farm with parents who wanted to protect him because of his deafness. We were in no doubt that, had he been born twenty years later, he would have found his voice, grown his intellect and created a fully independent life.

As I write these words, Geoff has been dead for two years, yet even today the mention of his name at St. Paul's Centre draws beaming smiles and tears. He lit up the place. Years earlier, when his mum died, his dad could not face the responsibility of looking after him, so without discussion or preparation took him to Cranage Hall and left him there. This scared Geoff, and instilled a fear that going away meant never coming back.

When we first met Geoff, he was living with the Lady Verdin Trust and edging towards the opportunity to live in his own place for the first time in life. Soon after, he did, moving into a flat with his own furniture and key to the door. Over the next five years, great effort was invested convincing him to take a holiday; this was a struggle, as he was sure that on return there would be no flat. Geoff did make the break, and eventually took to having more holidays than we could count. He went from enjoying a tentative one-night stop in a hotel, to long-haul flights and cruises.

Without speech or literacy, Geoff became our most reliable, helpful and industrious volunteer for nearly a decade. He became known for second-guessing everyone's next move. He often worked with me, making office space in the new business centre. After the first day, I learned to stay on the ladder and stretch out my hand. This was always met by the right tool, a hammer, screwdriver, nail or saw. Geoff would be there one minute and gone the next, only to re-appear with what he thought you would need next. Geoff had learned in life to read the world around him. He couldn't read a book but he could easily be the writer. Body language to Geoff was as descriptive as a computer manual to an IT expert.

As I reflect, I sense it cannot be right to comment on a person's capacity or ability before trying to extend or broaden it. "I must find a way to push this man and discover what more he can do," was something I often asked myself. I began to question if a person's limits are their environment, background or intellect. This I quickly abandoned to the psychology students, and focused on enriching the environment so Raymond, Geoff and others could try new things and be stretched.

In April 2014, a black horse-drawn hearse arrived at St. Paul's Centre. It was a scene that would not have looked out of place in the 19th Century. The coffin was carried through the main doors, borne on the shoulders of men who had worked alongside Geoff. With him, they had carried many wardrobes, beds and cupboards through the same doors, but on this day St. Paul's was returned to a congregational-style building for Geoff's funeral. Over 200 friends, family and colleagues came to celebrate a man who pulled a community together. In preparation for this day, all evidence that St. Paul's Centre housed furniture for reuse was removed.

Even in death, Geoff reminded us that St. Paul's Centre is not about the furniture.

## THE FEMININE TOUCH

David, a chap with a strange upbringing and even stranger profile in the Christian Bible, said, in an unusually serious moment: "My soul finds rest in God alone."

"Godalone! Is that a restful place far from here?" I asked myself, half joking. David summed up what it means to be in a position of responsibility when all around you seems difficult or harsh. He discovered that we must find for our soul, that inner self no other can truly know, a place of rest. Fortunately, I have known this for most of my life in leadership. However, there are moments when we all need the closeness of another human being. Such a person has been my constant companion and rescuer on many occasions.

My office door closed, I sobbed like a child alone on a beach filled with strangers. As the knot of sickly fear gripped my stomach, tears rolled down my face. "I can't take any more," were the words I cried to my wife. It was wonderful to have someone to turn to in a moment awash with more pain than words could express.

Seconds before this incident occurred, I was the Director in control, with the team looking to me for decisive and strong leadership in a difficult situation. Three young men in their early twenties wanted something we could not give, and they oozed with violent aggression. My response was, as ever, to protect my vulnerable staff, the interests of the charity and, sadly, not back down. In a flash, the biggest of the lads puffed up his chest, invaded my personal space, and firmly pushed his forehead on mine. I fully expected a broken nose!

I stood my ground and stared at him, with no love, acceptance or forgiveness in me. He backed off with threats to return. I encouraged everyone not to worry, and walked back into my office and collapsed. Some ten years later, I still saw him around town. We acknowledged each other, but we remained cautious of each other.

Over the past twenty years, my wife and I have been seeking to become broken bread, and we have poured out wine in our search to serve Jesus within the community. If, on the day mentioned above, I had received a broken nose, it would be a pain long healed by now, but the psychological damage done that day would have caused deeper scars than anything visible on my body. Deep incisions are inflicted on my soul, having been administered by the closest person, humanly speaking, to me - myself.

George Bernard Shaw said: "You see things; and you say, 'Why?' But I dream things that never were; and I say, 'Why not?'"

Without doubt, in the early days of my time at St. Paul's Centre, my head flooded with ideas and dreams about building stuff. A chance meeting with a drug addict, or broken man, would drive my thoughts for days. Hearing a problem was, to me, an invitation to find a solution. I drifted into too many unhealthy hours of work on occasions, which were failures to love my wife as I should have. If the Shaw comment was true of me, then the saying behind every successful man is a great woman would be easily applied to Cheryl, my wife. We are a balanced partnership in terms of skills and attitudes. Where I am extrovert and comfortable in public meetings, Cheryl likes quiet and obscure settings.

I titled this chapter 'The Feminine Touch' because, when I arrived in 1997, St. Paul's Centre was a masculine place – mainly blokes with boots grunting through life. This was reflected in the kind of activities and atmosphere around the site. There was a hardness and dysfunction about it. We, as a centre, were in crisis, and at the heart of the crisis was a gender imbalance. Not everyone will agree with this, but the evidence I point to is the sheer lack of women around.

A lady named Kath volunteered for the Friday sale. Kath was a dynamo of a woman, with a deep and authentic faith in God. She saw her time at St. Paul's Centre as an expression of her Christianity, an act of giving and serving. When it came to her leaving, I realised what a huge part she had played in keeping us going through the rebuilding and establishing of our place within the town.

A ship's captain may be on the deck looking ahead, but he can only do this with ease knowing there are loyal and committed engineers stoking the fire. Kath kept the sale going, regardless of the chaos around, giving me the space to not worry about it.

Overall, there were around 35 chaps working on the project, and two women - both for less than ten hours each week. Testosterone was in great supply. None of us had a clear sense of the gender imbalance, or the effect this had on the service being provided, yet we knew something was missing. I recognise there is a great deal of complex thinking on this subject, and some folk take offence at the nature of this discussion, but we needed to address this lack of female perspective.

Some twenty years on from that time of imbalance, our Director of Operations, Ali, would often refer to me as the honorary woman. She based this on her observation that I often see things through feminine, not masculine, eyes. Having grown up with three sisters, and having two daughters, has undoubtedly influenced my perspective.

There were some practical changes needed to make the site female friendly. One of the vulnerable adults working with us stood six feet four, and weighed 215 pounds. Like a stuck record, he would repeat words when he needed something. His passion was mopping floors, and for whatever reason the mop bucket was stored in the ladies' toilet. The door into the ladies had no lock, and once inside there were three cubicles each with broken locks. As one American visitor put it, "A rest room where you go in, and do what you need to, and get out with no rest time."

One morning, Cheryl was using cubical number three when the toilet door burst open, followed by the sound of "Bucket, bucket, bucket." She thought it best to sit tight, and stay quiet. He would probably be gone in seconds, once he had his bucket. The bucket was usually stored in the corner by the washbasin, but occasionally it was left in a cubicle. That day, a new word was added to the mantra, which now went "No bucket, no bucket, no bucket." This was followed by the first cubicle door being pushed open, with the kind of finesse that a giant would deliver.

BANG! "No bucket, no bucket, no bucket." Door two also revealed no bucket, but the attempt to open door three, forcibly, led to us bringing in a locksmith to make the ladies' loo more secure.

Around this time, I introduced some new administration staff, including several young trainees from local colleges. We also had some interesting people fulfilling their community service order: pay-back for crimes.

One of the team was a delightful and mature lady working in the office. Joy was kind and innocent in many ways, and from a Christian home. She carried an air of grace about her. This was visible in the way she walked, talked and sat. Her approach to work was of the utmost standard, filled with integrity, and she was scrupulous in her dealings.

One morning, a young man who had been placed in the office as he had an interest in administration, arrived late and fell asleep on the desk. "Didn't you get enough sleep last night?" Joy asked. "I was helping the police with an enquiry about a firearms incident until 4.00am," he told her. Several pairs of eyes appeared over the top of PC screens and then retreated. Within the space of twelve months, our team became an almost 50-50 split between male and female, including the decision makers. This was revolutionary in terms of ethos, values and approach.

Cheryl also began to come in and help around the centre, firstly looking at the bric-a-brac, clothing, bedding and anything that was not furniture. Raising children and working in nursing care had taught her that order must be brought on the road to gaining control. Cheryl knew that in the absence of an agreed process or leader, people would do as the book of Judges in the Old Testament puts it: "In those days Israel had no king; all the people did whatever seemed right in their own eyes." That is what we do; we respond from our own view of the world.

The mentality around the centre was, for some time, to focus on furniture – and the big items. Typically, the guys believed that if something was not hard to lift then it probably had little value. Some of the things that found a home in the waste bins were useful and valuable to us. Cheryl began to rescue and recycle stuff, and she built a team around the process. She enlisted new women volunteers and mothered them.

One major project development was a school uniform reuse project, and it attracted some great volunteers. First amongst the new recruits was Mary, a retired girls school head teacher. She had delightful, almost Victorian values, knew Latin and spoke of education as a doorway to the mysteries of life. Mary was passionate about removing barriers to learning, and the idea of offering virtually free uniforms to hard-pressed families appealed to her immensely. Her role was to pull the administration and paperwork elements together, and co-ordinate interaction with the schools. Had we put a plan together, and generated a person specification for the role, our dream candidate would have been Mary. Her vast knowledge of the school system, allied to her experience of being a head teacher, enabling her to establish dialogue with the right people, was vital to our success.

Twenty years on and we continue to have this same experience. In 2014, we began to explore the development of a new area of our work which involved young adults leaving full-time education. At the same time, as we applied for a grant to enable this work to grow, a local young woman contacted us. She had 14 years of experience as a primary school teacher and had decided to stop work and offer herself for voluntary work. Alexia and her husband were on a journey in search of a new life. Their prayers were in the form of questions, seeking an opening to give and work within the faith community. Like Mary in the late 90s, Alexia was the perfect match for the role we needed to fill.

Each time we have needed a person they have arrived. Many of the successful appointments at the charity have happened in this way. People and volunteers arrive at the most appropriate moment. Each time I sense the work of God, causing the paths of those we most need to cross with ours.

The Whole Child Project drew some exceptional people into the charity, many of whom migrated to other areas of work at the centre. Chris, who was a nursery nurse, came to help with the school uniforms and later took over the laundry. Her energy and speed of movement sent the guys running for cover. Chris was one of the women who saw something that needed doing, and just did it. She pulled together a team and began washing sheets and pillow cases, even the odd duvet. All this was done using domestic washing machines.

Around the time when Chris took charge of the laundry, we called it the Textile Project as it sounded better than laundry. We had a visit from the CEO of a local housing association (Wulvern Housing, now part of The Guinness Partnership), and during the tour of St. Paul's Centre I shared some stories about the people we helped. One of these stories concerned a small family struggling to keep the home together after a trauma. The mother and her three children were sleeping on the floor until our guys arrived with furniture, including beds. The guys who delivered the beds to the family returned to the centre saying that they felt terrible leaving the children with no bedding. They went back to the property within an hour with bedding and a few treats.

Standing in the organ loft, now our laundry room, Sue, the then CEO, said: "How many of these bedding packs go to our tenants?" I told her it was around 90%, and this included the family I had just mentioned. Through wet eyes she looked at Chris and the washing machine, and then turned to face me. "You need a better machine than this," she said. The following day, I received a call from an industrial washing machine company asking to arrange delivery and installation of a £4,000 machine.

Chris slowly took on different roles over the years, and continues to be a significant member of the team. Her speciality, and she would say privilege, is to manage all the furniture referrals. Chris kindly and graciously guides people around the centre as they choose furniture. Often, she listens to painful experiences of those who have arrived at a place in their lives where homelessness, loneliness and abandonment are crushing. Tea and tears are not uncommon at St. Paul's Centre.

The fact that teenage pregnancies were on the rise in Crewe inspired the development of baby boxes mentioned in a previous chapter. In turn, the school uniform recycling project came into being. Heather, a deeply spiritual woman, came to join the team running that scheme. Very quickly, it became clear that Heather had a yearning for a different kind of project. Her passion was to reach out to women experiencing crisis in pregnancy. Working with Heather, we managed to find and capture a fund to convert some of the mezzanine floor. This gave us a new office area, toilet, kitchen and counselling room. One thing invariably leads to another, and a new project came into being which we called The Kerith Centre. It was named after the Kerith Ravine, where Elijah the prophet was fed by ravens during a lonely and difficult time of isolation.

At the launch of the project, I was asked a question designed to entrap me: "Are you anti-abortion, Reverend Wykes?" My answer drew some negative comment. We discovered in those days the need to be clear about our aims in this project. The issue was simple to me. Whatever I was for or against was not the driver for the project. We were running a crisis pregnancy counselling service, not a campaign.

Over the few years that Kerith ran out of St. Paul's Centre, many women under tremendous pressure cried their way towards healing and wholeness. Not involved intimately with the counselling, I still became acquainted with some of the deeply painful stories. One sensitive and thoughtful lady in her 50s had spent 30 years wondering if the child she had aborted was a girl or boy, whether they would have become a doctor, office worker or a mechanic. Would she now have been a grandparent? Through encounter and support with crisis pregnancy services, this woman found release from a life of guilt. There were others with stories that broke our hearts.

St. Paul's Centre was the home for a satellite base for Sustrans, a national cycling charity located in Bristol. Our role, apart from landlord, included supplying secretarial support to Peter Foster, the regional manager of Sustrans.

One such person was Audrey Wilkin. Audrey arrived with a head full of lines from her favourite books and was an instant hit with the whole team. Aud, as she is known, breathed a beaming smile and worked with an air of complete competence. She was the first person I ever met who could type and talk and interrupt herself with the odd Jane Eyre quote. Lines such as "Do you think, because I am poor, obscure, plain and little, I am soulless and heartless?" would punctuate perfectly ordinary discussion. The office, the work and the people in St. Paul's Centre were greatly enriched by the presence of Aud.

After a few years working with us, Aud, like one of her other heroines, left to follow her dream. The road was not yellow-bricked, but paved with students and university lectures. She became a contemporary theatre and performance student which was of no surprise to the team. Before leaving, we had an outing to watch Aud in the local performance of 'The Liver Birds.'

That night, at the theatre, several of us sat together including a couple of the adults with learning difficulties. Geoff, whose hearing aids never seemed to work, and so his voice was not well regulated, sat with childlike anticipation. The moment Aud appeared on stage, Geoff let out a wolf whistle and shouted "That's that one from work." He was mesmerised by her costume and wig in the way so many children are when they realise Santa is really Uncle Tom or dad dressed up. About half way through the performance, Beryl, aka Aud, was ironing, and Geoff noticed the iron was not plugged in, so he let everyone in the audience know.

Aud completed her degree and did some acting and writing sketches but couldn't stay away. She returned to help set up St. Paul's Pantry, a food bank we as a charity run, which is housed in the organ loft where once we had a laundry. During her first year after returning to the team, she organised and coordinated the collection, packing and distribution of more than 12,000 meals for people who ate what they otherwise could not afford, and slept without the emptiness hunger brings. She did all this with energy, bounce and delivered many new lines gathered from her brief escape from the walls of St. Paul's Centre.

Filling the space that Aud left, there followed others; one had a Geordie accent and a cheeky smile, named June. St. Paul's Centre is where she began the journey from a long period of raising children, back into the world of work. From a sense of insecurity about being able to contribute, she became a major player in the success of the charity. She is the only person we have three names for in the personnel files!

In her early years with us, June faced a difficult, remarkable and sometimes dark journey that ended in a beautiful place in life. That has been true for others, such has been the space on offer at St.

Paul's Centre for those who came with great burdens and found a sense of belonging and rest.

June's capacity to focus and solve problems, linked to a refreshing work ethic, proved an asset. Sustrans moved out in early 2014, and June transferred to our reception. In this new role, she organised and captured data, and then helped to launch a new project which became a significant income generator. Like others in the charity, her ability to empathise, and a relentless pursuit to find good in people, ultimately led her to mentoring one of the young adults with special needs.

Can I invite you to use your imagination and picture a calm, ordered woman with the patience of Job? June could do the work in a tenth of the time on her own, but chooses to encourage, praise, direct and teach. The work is 'live' with real customers and part of her normal daily tasks, not an exercise without meaning or consequence. For most of us, we could do this for an hour once in a while, or as a teaching exercise. June has spent more than a year helping her young charge, never frustrated and always positive. She picks up the mistakes, and works extra quick to keep the work up to date.

During recognising the feminisation of the charity, it was clear, to those with a willingness to look, that finding a gender balance was one of the best developments to take place. There are books, articles, seminars and even laws seeking to qualify, encourage and even enforce what we found to be natural. It has been my privilege to discover and work with women who challenge my thinking and complement my character. Cheryl joining me at the beginning of my time leading the charity pushed on a door that unlocked the way for St. Paul's Centre to become a vibrant place, influenced by a feminine voice.

Our finance co-ordinator, Caroline, brought daily reminders to me of the difference, and yet similarity, of us as people. Caroline is German, and every now and then bursts into her mother language. I have no idea what she is saying. It could be from another planet. For us to work together, one of us must set aside our language for another's. Caroline does this graciously, but she doesn't stop being German. The idea that some work is for men and other work is for women is not true. But we do bring different attributes and character to our work. Somewhere in the mix of finding our way we stumbled on the richness of having a gender balanced community. The men have not given up being men, and women have not stopped being women, but we have learned to appreciate and respect our differences.

In the way that Caroline occasionally adopts another language to ensure good communication with whoever she is with, so we have grown to adapt. On occasion, we must all change language to ensure we give and receive the best opportunities.

## THE CHAPTER I DIDN'T WANT TO WRITE

The tea was cold and the mood was damp. Looking over my cup at the hands that held mine, I wondered which way to turn. The ring on Cheryl's delicate finger reminded me that I was not alone, and that others needed to be considered. We were sat in the window seat of the Big Apple Café in Crewe. Cheryl looked me in the eyes, and said: "Don't let this crush the life out of you, we can leave and start somewhere else."

It was John of the Cross who first wrote the phrase the *Dark Night of the Soul*, a poem in which he tells of the pain of loneliness and brokenness, and yet the joy of knowing God and the release such knowledge brings.

As a person, and especially as a community, for a few short but defining years we travelled through an experience that rocked our faith and tempted us to abandon the charity. We all have many parts of our life journey that we find hard to share, or sense it better not told. This was one of those. In short, we encountered an attack from quarters we least expected. Our name and integrity were challenged in a way that I believe was a dark and difficult time for the church in our town, and a poor reflection on our ancient and transforming faith.

I slipped the letter opener in and sliced the envelope open. The contents, a cheque book and paying-in book, looked like any other the bank sent us, except these were not from our bank - yet they carried our name. Being slightly dyslexic and always in a rush I did not notice, until it was pointed out that the envelope bore a name that was not Christian Concern Crewe, but one like the name. It was so similar that, for the next five years, postmen, delivery drivers, the public and most of the church could not get it right. A sophisticated and calculated set of public messages were used to divert resources from us to build a new shadow-like organisation. Subtle text changes gave maximum confusion to the public of Crewe.

This part of our history is one I did not want to tell but felt compelled to reveal. I say compelled because to not speak of it would be to remain quiet about the challenges we sometimes face when others of our own faith act on what appears to be flawed motivation.

"God told us," is a weak argument any follower of Christ can use when acting in a Christ-less manner. Skirting around this story, I found myself avoiding the questions from many people. "What about them over the road," they would say to me, or "Are you going to mention you know what?" was another.

This is not the last chapter in the book, but it was written after I thought all was complete, written following several prompts. One such nudge was a news item on the television in late summer 2016, which was embarrassing to the church as it once again brought disrepute on Christianity. There on the TV screen, convicted of a major fraud and deception of the benefit system, was the pastor of the group who this chapter is all about. I turned off the television, and said: "I cannot hide the part these people played in the journey of St. Paul's Centre."

It was a summer day, our annual open day in which we shared what the community at St. Paul's Centre were doing. Plans were laid out for new projects, people from all over the town came to support us, and one group of local Christians took a closer than normal look at the specifics of what we did. A promise of support and closer ties were mentioned. This was not to be. Within weeks, it became apparent that their intention was at best to copy, at worst to steal our great reputation.

Posted in the local newspaper was a small advert asking for unwanted furniture, with a phone number under the name of a local Pentecostal church. We had a good friendship with the pastor, and one of his congregation worked with us. It took less than fifteen minutes of conversation to recognise that the pastor felt overwhelmed and in a difficult place. He and some of the church hierarchy were sensitively trying to curb and control the activity of the man and his wife who were spearheading what they understood to be a one-off fundraiser. We discovered this person came with a history of causing disruption.

Over the next few weeks what unfolded was a masterpiece, and some will say a brilliant approach to marketing. A large building opposite St. Paul's Centre was rented and huge signs were erected. A two-page spread in the local newspaper was taken out to replace the small advert. Bear in mind the small advert was based on a church building nearby, and used the church phone number. The thrust of the new message spread across the newspaper's pages was simple: 'We have moved and changed our phone number.' This was true, but creatively the name used for this was Crewe Christian Centre. At the time, we were known as Crewe Christian Concern, often abbreviated to the 3Cs.

To test out how far this group was willing to go, we rang the number and asked if they were the furniture place on the corner of Hightown? With my own ears I heard "Yes, we are the church that people sometimes call the 3Cs."

From this moment on, we knew we had our work cut out. I wrote to the Charity Commission and challenged the name they were trading under. Feelings of guilt and betrayal came over me. The idea of having to turn to the secular authorities with a complaint about the behaviour of fellow Christians appalled me. I was not alone. Some well-meaning local Christian friends challenged me with comments about not accepting that God was in the new work. One even suggested we were less than Christian in not backing down and that we should consider closing for their sake, as they had prophetic anointing. Sense prevailed in small measure, as the Charity Commission wrote to them in April 2002 requesting that they change their name, emphasising that the name Crewe Christian Centre would not be permitted to the register.

Sadly, it took another five years to see any changes, a period, I felt, of humiliation for the church locally, as it struggled to avoid taking sides. On the surface, it looked like squabbling factions, but underneath a deeply spiritual battle raged.

The local press saw a story in it, and began to compare the two charities. Those running the counterfeit charity welcomed the publicity and gave a few interviews, whilst we refused to comment initially.

One week they placed a small but cutting advert in the local paper which came close to libel. It was a small list of comparison comments, one of which insinuated that our Trustees took money. I was personally embarrassed for them, as most had been good donors and none had ever taken a penny. Indeed, since I took over the charity in 1997, no Trustee has received any expenses.

I wrote to all the churches in Crewe expressing our sadness at the situation. Our concern was growing as the counterfeit charity began to rack up debts, and many of those they owed linked us to them because the names were hard to tell apart. In a bizarre twist, the water company connected our water charges together with theirs and began taking from our bank account funds to cover their service charges. Three months of letters and phone calls brought an apology and a refund from the water company, but no one else. The whole thing became embarrassing and hurtful.

This all took place between 2002 and 2006, and proved taxing on the whole team. As leader, holding the balance of voice was never easy for me. We had members of our team who were not professing Christians, and they could not understand why we refused to retaliate like-for-like. They saw injustice and wanted to retaliate through means they felt legitimate. At one point, we had some financial challenges and I had to take the team through a redundancy process. It was horrible. Sitting with your friends, and rationalising who you are letting go and why you have chosen them, was painful.

My heart twisted and turned and the nights were long and cold as I lay in bed wide awake feeling inadequate. Prayer was followed by bouts of anger. We had to tighten our belts and Christmas was near. There is never a good time to deal with difficult circumstances. We all took a small pay cut which meant most folk were on the most basic money you can earn. Cheryl and I worked out what we could reduce to lower our salaries, and it all worked out. I remember one of the team, a sensitive lady, with tears in her eyes, saying "None of us are in this for the money, are we Rob?" She was right of course.

In those days, we gave a Christmas card containing £10 to every member of the team, including the volunteers. This year, with money scares aplenty, Malcolm, our Chair, insisted on sitting with me and putting the money in the cards.

Traditionally, I write a personal note of thanks in each one, around seventy people in all. Malcolm felt it was important, for integrity reasons, that I did not put the charity's cash in envelopes on my own. He was right on the integrity front, but wrong on the cash. The charity didn't have the cash available that year, so Cheryl and I had used some funds from the re-mortgage of our house to fund the Christmas celebrations and some other small but needed bills to keep us all on the road. It was a genuine privilege to be able to do this, and God has shown us great kindness over the years during our life through the odd sacrifice.

Over the next few months, our small personal fund dwindled, and with it our little dream of a place to put a holiday caravan.

Then, one Wednesday morning, I opened the local newspaper to be greeted by a little advert placed by the counterfeit charity. There was the usual request asking for furniture donations, but with an extra box of text, outlined to draw attention, which read: 'Unlike some furniture charities we don't spend thousands of pounds on boss's wages.'

Sat at my desk I felt the rage of a madman run through my veins. For more than a minute I could not move for the beating of my heart was so fast. My emotions were out of control, and I knew it. I switched on the computer and created a new document, and began to write my resignation.

'I have enjoyed my time leading the charity and feel it is now time to…'

An hour later the document was deleted and I was on my knees, literally on my knees praying. In that moment, I was reminded that God is our provider and our trust, reputation and future are in His hands.

These were valuable lessons for us as a charity, and in the following years many of the challenges we faced would be measured against these experiences. We discovered that very few of the conflicts we encountered with individuals or organisations were personal. We realised that a bigger picture exists, of which we play a small part.

Looking back, we recognised how valuable adversity is, for without it our resolve and commitment are not tested. We all need a healthy balance of tension in what we do. There is a helpful image in the New Testament which speaks of living a life of faith as though it were a race. The writer says '…Run the race that we have to run with patience, our eyes fixed on Jesus the source and the goal of our faith.'

Through what I can only describe as our dark night of the soul, we learned the rich truth that all medal-winning Olympians know; we learned to focus on the goal set before us, neither looking left or right, but straight ahead.

## A BOLT OF LIGHTNING AND AN EARTH ROD

One of the fascinating dynamics around St. Paul's Centre has always been the diverse collection of people. They come in all shapes and sizes, and talk in many dialects. They are usually busy doing practical things, and always seem to have an agenda. Somehow, the collective fits together perfectly despite some being strong, dominant characters, while others sit in the background, hardly muttering a word.

We all have an agenda – an idea of how best things should be done. Over the years, St. Paul's Centre has drawn in articulate, educated professionals who got stuck in alongside working class and long-term, often poorly educated, unemployed folk. Many on both sides were broken in spirit, yet kind in heart and energetic in the good deeds they did.

There have been times when the mix was not right, and the result can be terrifying. In fact, we have never had a shortage of people who thought the answer, regardless of the question, could be delivered via the fist! In equal measure were folk who thought those with poor education had chosen to be that way. At this point you must have worked out that St. Paul's Centre is not Heaven, and the community within it is not made up of angelic beings faultlessly serving one another.

The social gap was so wide, that on one occasion at our annual Christmas chip lunch, there was a man who lived under a nearby bridge sat next to a lady who lived in the richest part of town. Somehow, they got on and shared our diversity. On reflection, we would not be who we are without this incredible spread of wonderfully different people getting along with each other.

Charities, businesses or organisations of any configuration need to have a balanced team. There are books and seminars and gurus aplenty lining the 'How To Make It A Success' highway, selling the latest and most innovative ideas about team make-up and dynamics. Over many years, I have sought out some of these offers and considered the touted wisdom. However, nothing can compensate for working hard at developing relationships and learning to play a part in the unfolding drama of where we labour. How boring the world would be if we were all the same!

Gathering people of different abilities and character from a vast array of life experiences can be exhilarating. If your role, like mine was, is to hold these together, at the right tension, to gain the best from the gathered mass, then you need those you lead to have a healthy respect for you. Left alone, people with vastly differing experiences and ideologies can create carnage.

Let me share my experience about two very different people, who, in an unplanned way, brought a balanced growth spurt to the work at St. Paul's Centre, at a time when it could have all easily collapsed.

First, Stephanie. With a stern look and barely visible smile she drew my name out for several seconds – ROBBEERRT! I knew in an instant; like the little boy pinching a biscuit before tea, I had been rumbled. I have always been partial to sarcasm, or to vocalising my frustration, and suddenly this was challenged.

We all need people in our lives that have permission to challenge us. We must choose to give that permission, and then live with the consequences. I found in leadership that being open to challenge is a delicate business. My weakness is not lack of action, more often the opposite. Another weakness has been my passion for the community of St. Paul's Centre; criticise that at your peril.

In 2002, this young German woman called Stephanie entered the charity, bringing with her a view of the world which, on the surface, seemed complex and overthought. However, Stephanie saw through a great deal of the games people play and managed to get to the heart of what motivates us. Every time I slipped into sarcasm, or over-vented my thoughts about a person or situation, Steph would bring me back to earth with a "ROBBEERRT" that would stop me in my tracks. This was a throwback to my childhood as I have been known as Rob for most of my life, never Bob. In my younger days, however, my mother would call me Robert when I needed to be chastised. In a flash, I was eight years old again.

Stephanie was not the first person to work at St. Paul's Centre who challenged me to a higher expression of my faith, but Stephanie left an enduring reminder of the centrality of our Christian heritage and core reason for being.

Standing in the white goods workshop some years after Steph had left the charity, I went to great lengths to explain to a group of young visitors the need for an earth rod. The purpose of such a device is, I went on to explain, to offer a path to dissipate a static discharge, such as lightning. Without this, electricity has nowhere to go, and if struck by it we might fry.

Over a seven-year period, Steph became an earth rod to me. She challenged and deflected many of the fiery darts that headed my way. When one landed, she stepped in and reminded me to stay on message. I sensed she did this all unintentionally.

Her own journey to St. Paul's Centre was remarkable. From Germany, she travelled to Florida to study, later coming to Crewe as a missionary based with West Street Baptist Church. Stephanie first encountered St. Paul's Centre when she joined a local group on a visit, and later having a prayer meeting in the centre.

"At first, I was a bit side-tracked by the fact that something I perceived in my German mind to be a business was taking place in God's house. You have to forgive me for that; you see, in Germany the concept of charitable work does not really exist, even less the concept of furniture redistribution - you hold on to it until it is kaput!" Stephanie went on to say how, as she prayed around St. Paul's Centre, her heart was moved and the Holy Spirit showed her this was God's work.

A year or so after this, and whilst working to make ends meet in ASDA on the tills (which in Christian circles is called tent making, although ASDA call it working on the tills), Stephanie encountered Cheryl, my wife. Stephanie was on her way to the job centre, hoping to find another way to pay the bills. Cheryl asked her if she could type, to which came the reply "Of course, and with all ten fingers."

Days later, in early February, 2004, Stephanie joined the team as a part-time secretary, supplied by us to one of the tenants at St. Paul's Centre, called Sustrans. In a short time, I discovered Stephanie to be a deeply spiritual person with a powerful drive to serve others. She read the Bible from end to end regularly, and made me feel uncomfortably unspiritual. She had the kind of faith or trust in God that was disarming, naïve to some minds but refreshing to others.

Looking back, it is a miracle that she rose above my cynical and sarcastic commentary on life, to eventually love me as a friend. Across my first two decades at the centre, she is one of only a handful of people who truly got what I saw as a calling to develop and minister Christian practical love through St. Paul's Centre.

Stephanie brought a constant reminder of the deeper view of life, and a gracious commentary to accompany it. She read and often recalled the most obscure details of the C.S. Lewis *Narnia* tales. We joked that Steph could quote huge passages from the vast texts, and that she spoke as though Narnia and the characters within the stories were real. For a short while, she lived in our family home during a time when our youngest daughter was hitting her late teens. Over a period of one year, I ate my meals sandwiched between Florence Nightingale and Amy Winehouse.

Through a series of unplanned and not-well-managed changes to the structure of the charity, Stephanie became my PA. She loved to organise things into rows, lines and structures. Lean systems-style thinking could have been her brainchild, and I found great comfort in having someone around me pressing order into my busyness. In truth, she became my manager and has never been replaced. Years after she had left we welcomed an Operations Director, Ali. Following the revelation that something was out of place, she used to say: "Don't tell me – it didn't happen when Stephanie was here!"

In many ways, Ali did pick up the major part that Stephanie played in the charity, for she brought us back to the centre of our faith expression. She also picked up the baton of challenging me when I was consumed with cynicism.

The truth is that Stephanie was not perfect, as none of us are, but she cared deeply about what really mattered to the charity at the time. She set a standard – unattainable in part, but worthy of reaching for. She reminded us that being a Christian organisation meant acknowledging God as the arbiter in our relationships, standards and, ultimately, the one to whom our efforts are offered.

Against the back-drop of this innocent, gentle, organised, Germanic, measured and well-designed administration that Steph brought, entered Colin.

Colin was different! Sports cars, gold watches and a large house were a thing of the past for Colin when he walked through the door of my office. His stance and smile ushered a sense of energy and excitement into the room. Whilst I had heard the saying nervous energy, until this moment I had not truly encountered anyone with such fire burning within.

For much of the time at the centre, we worked with people walking a lonely road and carrying a heavy sadness – the signs of depression or disappointment all too apparent. Most of my energy was taken up pushing and encouraging people to take a risk, and to develop confidence, but in Colin I met someone for whom my time would be spent holding him back, often pouring water to dampen his flames. He was a bolt of lightning, and left unchecked he stirred in me the wildest dreams, usually encouraging entrepreneurial risk-taking.

Colin was a charmer who shook your hand firmly and always touched your shoulder, a man of real passion with a mind that raced at 90 miles per hour. When he joined us, Stephanie was effectively my PA. She was calm in approach, logical in thought, and deeply spiritual in heart. She was a guardian of the spiritual tempo, concerned for the Christian presentation of the charity's work. She was feminine and sensitive in character. Colin was a man's man who enjoyed banter and dealt head on with the guys.

In life, we come across people who only share the briefest leg of their journey with us, but you still think "Wow" that person's story would make a great book. Colin was one of them, and maybe his book will appear one day. He was a local Crewe man who had run several businesses, and possibly had a similar number of wives during that time. Something of an action man, he skied, rode horses and collected expensive watches. He also lost much of what he had, on more than one occasion! Colin came to St. Paul's Centre on his way back up, after a particularly difficult business collapse and a family break-up. He had lived on a knife-edge for some time, and he was ready to come in from the cold. I have no doubt that, in many ways, for Colin it was like stepping off a sinking raft onto dry land when he walked into St. Paul's Centre.

The moment I met Colin, I took a shine to him; and in the second moment, I wondered how we could bring him into the team. He was one of those people you put in a room with a blank sheet of paper and he would come out with a plan to change the world. It would be wrong to say that everyone understood him, but there is no doubting that anyone who met the man never forgot him.

From where I stood, Stephanie and Colin could not have been any more different, and yet they were perfect additions to the team that allowed us to move forward. They were never destined to be close friends outside the charity, but they respected each other and worked for the good of the charity and those we served.

So, why have I picked these two team members, and what part of the overall story do they enhance or illustrate?

When Colin arrived, we had travelled through a difficult and dark time. Our position in the community had been challenged, and our board and I had endured much criticism. The decision to not enter the press game, making counter comments to those who pointed accusing fingers, sounded easy and right, but it was hard. On a personal level, Cheryl, as my wife, was the only person to witness the true toll it all took on my emotions and confidence.

Stephanie gave me daily encouragement to trust the Lord. There was no end to the flow of Bible verses she quoted. We were now at the exit point to all this discomfort, and looking back it was the beginning of a time of blessing for the charity.

Just before Colin's arrival, the charity had been blessed with surplus income. This allowed us to plan and implement positive change to the physical structure of St. Paul's Centre. The old church building had its pros and cons, nothing pretty about the space really, but very utilitarian. So, Colin was unleashed and he set about affecting some dramatic changes. He installed industrial racking on the mezzanine floor, and transformed the areas outside the building with metal containers and roofing to create dry storage.

What Colin brought was excitement and camaraderie. Each time I walked out into the centre to see how things were going there was always laughter and fun. Before he joined the team, I understand there were moments of deep darkness and little laughter. The building was also cold, and for some time Colin suggested that a wood burner could resolve the issue of dipping temperatures during the winter months.

The idea to install such a system also ticked other boxes. We did weekly trips to the waste tip, taking old wardrobes or wooden furniture that didn't make it to needy households or the weekly sale. That always seemed such a shame. A furniture project nearby had a wood burner and piped the warm air around their building. So, making better use of our surplus and unwanted stock seemed like a great idea, and Colin was the right man to begin investigating our options. I thought that £10,000 would do it; he had other ideas.

One cold, February morning we set off to look at a system that Colin had found following several weeks researching the subject. When we arrived, at an impressive industrial unit, my jaw nearly hit the floor. The wood-burning system that greeted us was amazing, a massive chipper to shred wood, a hopper to swirl and separate the chips, and a conveyor belt to take the fuel up to the wood burner. The system was so efficient, the staff wore shorts in the winter. Unfortunately, this deluxe solution would have cost us £60,000 plus VAT. Colin now had me thinking big, so I bought some warmer jackets for the chaps back at the centre!

If Colin and I were left alone, it was like having a car with two accelerators and no brakes. I think we both knew that the charity was a place for Colin to rest and recharge his batteries, and yet he never rested. During his time with us, we converted the church hall which later became the John Ashe Hall. On one occasion, he and I were on ladders removing some timber studding. Colin reached over to remove a screw, he over-stretched and started to pass me on his way to the floor, but I luckily managed to grab him. It was a Laurel and Hardy moment, a reminder that we were not sitting in an office talking about developments, but up ladders making changes. Fortunately, Colin was responsible for Health & Safety and had no one else to blame. This was another lesson I learned along the way – risk is part of growth, and budgets didn't always allow for bringing in outside help.

The day I instinctively knew would arrive, did eventually come. Colin asked for a quiet word. "I love it here," he told me, "and I wish I could stay for ever, but I need more flexibility than you can give me." He went on to outline his plan for the next phase of his life, which included a three-month intensive course to become a heating engineer. You can still see his van around the town with SPS on the side (Specialist Plumbing Services).

Not long after this, Stephanie left to work in Israel and later moved home to Germany where she married a great American guy she met in Jerusalem. Her influence on the charity's approach to administration and spirituality continues to this day.

I called this chapter 'A Bolt of Lightning and an Earth Rod' because of Colin and Stephanie; he came at the right time to give us a jolt. He was a whirlwind of energy, ideas and chaos - all of it fun. The reference to an earth rod was, of course, about Stephanie. She brought order and sanity, not dullness - far from it. In Stephanie I rediscovered my place in the charity, and in Colin I was reminded to act and energise the team. In their own separate ways, they contributed to the longevity and vitality of St. Paul's Centre.

## ENDURING SUPPORT

Sliding my hand across the smooth surface of the luxurious desktop, I began to understand the comment made in reception. As I waited to be collected from the waiting area of the world's most famous motor car manufacturer, a man in overalls had said: "You're off to Mahogany Row, are you?"

Hidden beneath his question was a minor jealousy, as Mahogany Row was, and still is I believe, the suite of offices occupied by the board of directors at Rolls-Royce (now Bentley Motors). To my great surprise, Sheila, one of my neighbours, appeared in reception to collect me. Her house was a few doors down the same street where I lived. It was news to me that she worked at Rolls-Royce, let alone as the personal assistant to the Director of Human Resources, Christine Gaskill.

The quality and feel of the place oozed perfection. The desk in reception was matched by beautiful chairs in the waiting area, with bespoke furnishings to match. It was a far cry from my second-hand desk, and makeshift chair that lost a wheel every time I stood up.

Christine was tall, extremely smart in her formal dress, and carried an air of being in control. I was there to talk about our charity, but for a moment I froze. Sitting on the other side of that imposing desk, looking very important, she transported me instantly to a distant childhood memory.

Mr. Innes, my school headmaster, once invited me to sit opposite him, at his old and polished-to-death mahogany desk, keen to explore my bad behaviour. He gave me a plate with two biscuits, accompanied by a glass of orange squash. I took the first biscuit and crunched. It was a good way to deal with trouble, I thought, all very civilized. Then, reaching across the table, he slid the plate away from me.

"This will hurt me Wykes, and it disturbs me to have to do this," he said, as the mood quickly changed. The tension in the room rose, and I knew we were moving from an adult discussion to something more painful.

What happened next would be illegal nowadays. He stood and walked round the desk, carefully picking up his metre-long flexible cane.

I was invited to touch my toes and stand still. The first strike landed high on the curve of my backside. The pain made me jump up, and I rubbed the damaged area furiously. The next blow was a direct hit, like the second bowl on the cricket field; Mr. Innes now had his eye in.

Fortunately, my punishment was only two strokes. "Sit down and finish your biscuit, lad," he said, as he returned to his side of the desk. During the whole process, he didn't raise or lower his voice, display anger or disappointment. It was all very professional. I, on the other hand, nursed a fire that raged in my pants as I sat most uncomfortably to finish that unwanted biscuit.

The memory of this encounter has stayed with me, and was rekindled as I looked across that polished mahogany desk at someone else obviously in control. Thankfully, Christine was nothing like Mr. Innes. Instead of enduring punishment, I excitedly shared my vision of St. Paul's Centre with one of Rolls-Royce's senior executives. It was almost impossible to be calm in those early days, as my passion for the cause raced through my veins. Articulation of my ideas was a challenge, because my comfort zone was preaching; I told people things.

Mid-flow, with my arms flailing, Christine interrupted: "Graham also needs to meet you." I had no idea who Graham was, but moments later Graham did meet me. He was the Chief Executive of Rolls-Royce. The ante-room to his office was better furnished and more comfortable than our lounge at home. The coffee was nice, but cool enough so that the impromptu meeting was not prolonged too much. That he was in the building, in his office, and in the mood to meet an unknown chap for an unplanned conversation, was confirmation of God's omni-something or other. Graham listened whilst looking at me, undistracted by his busy schedule and importance to the car industry.

You learn a lot from brief encounters with people in high places. Graham's accent gave him away instantly; his mother tongue brought the Beatles to mind, and ferries across the Mersey. Interrupting, his PA apologetically advised us that we needed to draw a close on the meeting. Graham told me he wanted to hear more. "Christine will be in touch," were his parting words. I left the building not sure if this would lead to anything, but encouraged that I had been heard.

The entrance to St. Paul's Centre in those days was through two solid wooden doors. Inside, it was rectangular with five doorways; the lobby was under-used and awkward in shape. To the right was a door to the church hall, now known as John Ashe Hall. It was a mish-mash of accommodation, and to host our guests from Rolls-Royce we needed to create something.

Hastily, we built a stud partition cutting off a section of the lobby. Magnolia paint was used to cover the bare brick walls, with the addition of some donated pictures, although this was not Mahogany Row! Our budget of £40, and two days to complete the task, had created a conference room the size of a postage stamp. Miraculously, we found six matching chairs not unlike the small coffee table we had placed in the middle, upon which sat the overhead projector.

"They're here," shouted Joy, our finance person, as she peered through a window on the morning of their visit. In the fashion of a wedding group stood in line receiving their guests, we stood at the entrance as a welcoming party. The prestigious minibus drew up, and the Board of Rolls-Royce alighted. Stood before us were an array of shiny cufflinks and high heels, but not on the same people! We had an hour to convince them we were worth an investment. Could we inspire them to join us along some of the journey?

Slowly, and carefully, I walked them through those words, laying emotional foundations first, followed by practical needs. "Come and see what I mean," I then said, my signal to show them what St. Paul's Centre was all about.

We toured the building so they could meet real people and hear real stories. It was interesting to see the reaction of our guys at the centre. Barriers of prejudice and ignorance rose, echoes of a working-class response to the bosses who walked amongst them.

Moving around the building the stories were rolled out. A key theme was unemployment and lack of opportunity. We needed them to move beyond knowing that local people needed a job, to knowing the people by name. Sat in the small, cramped, newly-painted conference room, on the screen I flashed up for the first time the words that defined the charity – hope, dignity, confidence and opportunity.

As they left, Graham shook my hand. "Christine will be in touch," he said, the now somewhat predictable finish to our meetings. He was true to his word, and she was in touch, initiating a second visit to the wonderful Mahogany Row.

Reflection on memory is a wonderful thing. For some the memory is a vague mist with little detail, unless there is significance in the original encounter. We were in a moment of collision with Rolls-Royce and they were a team who got what we were about.

On our follow-up visit, organised by Christine, we were given two gifts. The first was a cheque for £5,000, a genuinely useful sum at a time of famine for us. Of course, the money also meant public identification with the charity, which came to be a great help. The second gift was an introduction to a young chap completing an MBA in business management. It was arranged for him to visit St. Paul's Centre and meet us. I must confess to fearing we had been given a wet-behind-the-ears consultant, or worse, someone who thought they were God's gift to the world of business coaching.

As you read this book there will be people in your life who have been there for a significant moment. "They helped shape my thinking, and pointed me in the right direction," is something you may say about some of those people.

In church life people have what is called a spiritual mentor or director. This may be someone who listens and shares their wisdom, or reflects what you say to help shape your thoughts and decisions. In the past 30 years, there has been a growth of professional mentors or lifestyle coaches. Books are followed by seminars which offer ongoing guidance. Sizeable companies have departments that specialise in developing their staff for better performance. The man Rolls-Royce sent was not like that.

"Did you say Williams, Robbie Williams?" I asked. "I wish," came the reply. "It's Lightfoot, Robbie Lightfoot," he confirmed.

This was my first encounter with a young man who would revolutionise the way we thought about the charity's operation. Many of the thinking processes that now take place at St. Paul's Centre are due in a large part to the gift they gave us that day. Robbie became part of the team over the subsequent years. Occasionally, he would help with specific members of the team, with coaching or with team dynamics. He moved from Rolls-Royce to work at a university, followed by a utilities company, and eventually working for himself running a coaching and management consultancy business.

St. Paul's Centre was never an experiment, or a poor placement for Robbie. He didn't do his allotted time and then move on. Robbie took the work to heart and grew a vision of his own. The value of his input is clear to see in the way we communicate today, how we now write business plans, how we structure team gatherings and measure what we do. There is also a hidden value to his support of the charity, for every six weeks or so he continues to meet with me, challenging and encouraging, drawing out and reflecting on my thinking. He hid well any frustration with our sometimes-slow march towards organisational excellence. He always grasped the budget constraints and the personal choices we made. Robbie understood that we don't always choose the best person for a role, but the person who would benefit most from an opportunity.

Robbie taught me how to write learning logs and smile at my own failures. On more than one occasion, I would relate a difficult situation with a member of the team who hadn't worked out. One example comes to mind. At every turn this chap fell short on the job. I would patch things up, fill in the gaps and set him off again. A week later, there would be another problem. Eventually, everyone was screaming at me to deal with it and let him go.

The next time I saw Robbie, he said: "You knew this before you took him on." It's true, I did. My heart makes more decisions than my head, and thus we have brought into the team many people who couldn't deliver. However, some have – and to me that would make it worthwhile. One success comes to mind. David, who had once been with us for six months, was working at the job centre advising and supporting people on long-term sickness benefits. His role was to help them explore their options and move towards a phased return to work. He would set them up with a volunteering position initially, and then grow their capacity and resilience ready for paid employment. A young man named Phil was on his radar. He instantly liked him, and he could see something in him that others could not. They arranged to visit me, and I shared the same sense that Phil had something about him.

Phil came along tentatively for a few half-days, all afternoons, as he was not good in the mornings. During an off-the-cuff conversation with Phil, he told me that he had a full, clean driving licence. He was willing to drive the van, and we always needed drivers.

Around the same time, we had been talking to the local council about dove-tailing with some of their collections from local households. These were special pick-ups of items that didn't fit into the standard domestic wheelie bins. Members of the public paid a small fee to have furniture and other large items taken away, often to the tip. Our aim was to cherry pick anything re-useable. We established an agreement to conduct a pilot scheme which, in charity language, means that if it fails nobody gets the blame.

To make this happen, we needed a regular driver. So, I gave a presentation to the Rotary Club in Nantwich, seeking funds to kick-start our idea. Following an impassioned talk about our work, and the people we served, I said: "At St. Paul's Centre, we have a young man that none of you would call for interview, or employ, because of his fall from grace. I will employ him on your behalf."

I recall the many faces looking at me, acknowledging that they truly would not employ Phil. Thankfully, the first to respond to my heartfelt appeal was Graham Tresidder, a local funeral director and a man with the kindest face I had ever seen. He said: "How much do you need?" With his encouragement, and the collective support of the other businessmen, I cycled back to Crewe with six months' wages for our new driver.

Phil's past life included an encounter with drugs, and a long period of estrangement from his family. At the time of our meeting, he was making a break for normal life. He was moving cautiously towards the centre and away from the margins of society. I wanted to give him a paid job and, in some ways, bring him in from the cold.

The snag was his medication. Methadone (a prescribed drug) is something the DVLA require you to declare. I explained to Phil that our insurance wouldn't cover us if he didn't declare this. However, his CDT (Community Drugs Team) support worker advised him against this. The CDT officer told him of others who had had their licence taken away after making the declaration. He told Phil it was an advisory rule, not a law of requirement. We couldn't risk it. "If you do the right thing, the right thing will happen," I said to Phil, sat in my office one afternoon.

My confidence was such that I reassured Phil that whatever happened I would still employ him for six months, driving the van myself if necessary. Days later, Phil sat in my office downbeat and annoyed with me. The DVLA had revoked his licence following the declaration of his medication. It was a struggle remaining positive as my heart listened as he challenged me. "You said if I do the right thing, the right thing will happen," he said, repeating my words. I felt sick, and he felt sick.

We appealed the decision, and they granted a short-term temporary licence with conditions attached. Over the following few years, Phil regularly went to the doctor for drug testing, and filled in forms for his next temporary licence. Eventually, they gave in and reinstated his full licence. Phil had left his old life behind and proved the authorities wrong.

In my office, there are lists of wonderful, remarkable and resilient people. Their lives have been the embodiment of the vision God, I believe, set out before me in 1997, the same vision he set out before John McCallum in 1986, and before John Ashe in 1868. These are people for whom the promise of prophet Isaiah has come true: "Won't the God of all the earth do the right thing?"

Phil continues to drive, and he is our best driver to date. I pray that one day one of those businessmen who funded his first six months at St. Paul's Centre will pay him more than we can afford, and take him on to greater things.

Space does not permit me to talk at length of Malcom or Bill, who now run their own businesses having rested with us for a while.

There was also Lee and Ted, who moved back to significant roles in management. I must not forget Tracy, who went on to raise a family and spread her beaming smile across the town; or Joy, now working for a mission, and changing lives by the day.

Through all this and more, 'Rolls-Royce Robbie' (as I always called him) has faithfully visited, encouraged and mentored me. One year we all went to a local church, where Robbie helped profile the team. We explored our differing skill bases and ways of learning. We just had time to discover who was good at what, and the best way to make the most of the team when half of them left. Those who remained slotted into what was needed, not what was best for our skill set.

Looking back, I did not see Robbie's workshop and our search for a closer team wasted, I sensed that this was a timely reminder of our dependence on God, not systems and best practice. There it is again: Trust in God's omni-something. Such is the dynamic of our little charity at St. Paul's Centre, it is a community within seeking to influence the community outside. The internal balance of our gathering, though ever changing, is maintained by faith and work.

Through reflection, and with the help of Robbie, I have learned that historic knowledge is invaluable. Our gift has been the challenge of the transient populace of St. Paul's Centre asking "Why do it that way?" or "Can we change it?" set against the old timers' experience of Chris, Cheryl, Phil and Peter.

"We've seen it before," is something we might say, having been around for several decades. For others, their fresh take on things, and willingness to try new ideas, is a tremendous blessing.

## THE CHAIR AND ITS OCCUPANTS

Over the past twenty years, we have had six Chairs, enough for a dining set, if such were the chairs of which we speak. The role of Chairperson is not to be taken lightly, or with disregard for its seriousness and importance in the life a charity. One of our Trustees held this responsibility for more than fifteen of the twenty years I have been CEO. Our experience as a team has been one of full support from the board, with no Chair stepping down or leaving through disagreement or disharmony. The spirituality and prayerful life of the board has been a major contributory factor in blessing and success of the work.

Pam was the Chair of Trustees when I was invited to lead the charity. She lived in Birmingham, which was in many ways impractical. Pam was part of the original charity called Teamwork, who gave the legal covering to the initial group that set up Crewe Christian Concern in 1987. Jamie, Pam's husband, was an integral part of the work at St. Paul's Centre in the late 1980s and early 90s. He had an eye for quality furniture that had been donated to raise income. He knew about restoration, mostly of people but also in good measure about old furniture. Once I had taken the reins, and a couple of new local Trustees joined the board, Pam stepped back.

During the first days of my leadership, Pam gave some insightful and encouraging words. She stepped off the board in a gracious manner having dealt with the uncomfortable moments of my predecessors moving on. Together we faced the challenges of steering the charity in a new direction. I used to joke with Pam that we really should have an Anglican vicar for Chair, and when she asked why I simply said: "It would look good." In truth, I sensed a need within me to have a serving minister as my spiritual oversight and champion on the board.

From the outset, I believed that I'd had a calling to be a minister, not a manager. In my heart, I wanted a Chair that saw me in that light, challenged me in that light and prayed for me in that light. An inner voice, and the experience of Christian ministry, informed me that keeping a leader in touch with, and challenged to have, a vibrant and reflective personal faith, would be sufficient to safeguard the charity. Lodged with the Charity Commission under the title 'Aims of the charity' are the words "The advancement of the Christian faith," which was, and should remain, our starting place. I believed the charity would be well served in this if the leadership had a sense of vocation like that of a church leadership.

Striving for integrity as an expression of our faith, and operating the charity in line with this core aim, demanded that we view ourselves through the correct prism. In those early days, I had sensed the need for the whole charity to be challenged as a faith expression. This, I believed, needed to start at the top and work its way down. At board level, it was important that we had a clear sense of our Christian heritage. To enable this kind of reflection in our discussions, our meetings began with one board member bringing a thought from the Bible. We found this set the tone and developed the platform from which to build our thinking.

St. Paul's Centre is not a church in the traditional sense any longer but, this we always believed, should never inhibit our desire to be shaped and modelled by a communal faith encounter. It was tongue in cheek that I wanted an Anglican vicar as Chair, but this served as a good metaphor. Our need was spiritual leadership, and we held that attribute as highly as fiscal or managerial skills required to lead the charity.

Pam was followed by Tim Saunders, not an Anglican vicar, but a devout Christian from a local church, with scrupulous values and high standards of expectation. I recall Tim, at our first one-to-one meeting, arriving with a cream cake. He said: "Get that artery blocker down ya." He worked for a large pharmaceutical company developing new drugs, and I have no doubt some of the treatments were designed to lower cholesterol. Tim had a sense of humour.

Tim became a lifelong friend to the community at St. Paul's Centre, and although he is now halfway around the world, he regularly enquires about us and visits the centre when on UK soil. He is one of those remarkable people who can learn something new very quickly. A pharmacist by trade, and a leader by nature, he was kind and committed. At the time of his joining the board, Tim was in the process of negotiating the introduction of an eye ointment to the American market. Eating my artery-clogging cake, I listened to Tim share the complexity of working to satisfy the American food and drug administration. He spoke of this in a fun and interesting way, although I am confident that it wasn't as simple as filling out a form and sending the registration cheque.

In Tim, I quickly came to recognise what a real asset God had placed before us. In one meeting with him, when trying to explain my lack of formal education (that I was functionally illiterate), it was apparent that he wasn't interested. He said: "Good, now you know what you can't do, find someone who can." Don't misinterpret that, as Tim had great respect for me and flung himself into supporting me in my role. Still, what I couldn't do was of less importance than what I could do. He believed in people and understood the dynamic of how teams play to a group member's individual strength.

Tim taught us how to pool what we had, and how to formulate a goal as a collective aim. I recall some of the team's eyes glazing over when, under Tim's guidance, we began process mapping. Pete, one of our collection team drivers, challenged every step of writing or recording the process. His distrust hindered any progress. Recognising that we were in danger of this development being undermined, I remember asking Pete what his problem was. His response revealed so much of the reason he was a long-term unemployed man with a terrible record of not sticking at jobs. "It's a great idea for everyone else to follow," he said, before going on to tell me he liked a more flexible approach to tasks. Pete eventually accepted that he was not a team player, or a community-minded person. Try as we might, he just didn't want to work in a prescribed way.

With Tim's help we began to learn how to deal with real issues and they don't come much more real than a grumpy, difficult and obstructive team member. This is where our faith was put under the spotlight. That God loved the people we were working with was never in doubt, but their fit in the team was. A phrase I use in churches when speaking was developed in the furnace of managing challenging people: "It is easy to be a Christian on Sunday, but occasionally painful on a Monday." Standing each morning with the team, it is nice to pray for God's blessing on the tasks of the day ahead. They are nice prayers, unless the "Amen" is followed by "Would you come to my office Jenny, for a chat about a performance issue." Not all tasks are easy or nice, no matter how much prayer you put into it.

In those days, we had a delightful and faithful saint of a man, David, who acted as bookkeeper. He had been working in a bank until the introduction of calculators, and he refused to use one. The computer was the last straw, so he left banking. He simply didn't understand why you needed technology. Tim and I sat mesmerised watching David run his pencil down a list of more than 50 individual figures, all four or six digits long. Consequently, all our financial records were on large, lined sheets in columns of red, blue and green ink. The data was accurate to the decimal point, and meticulous in its recording, but it was useless for analysis or profiling. We needed change, but David wasn't budging and we were not pushing. Tim and I agreed to get a recognised accounting package.

When the software arrived, none of us in the office had a clue how to use it, but Tim arrived one evening after work and took the computer and the new package home. I wrote a list of headings denoting the way I wanted to separate the income and expenditure streams. The following morning, Tim returned with the package loaded, configured and with a set of his own written instructions.

Yes, but how good was the set-up I hear you ask? Today, 20 years on, we still use that same list of headings, and we have never lost a penny of the £6m that has travelled through the books.

For a couple of years, we ran the two systems: David and a paper version, with Joy, one of the new team members, running the computerised accounts. We managed to find ways to keep David working for the charity until his deteriorating health forced him to retire.

The significance of Tim as Chair was timing and talent. He was a process-driven man who, in his day job, recorded and tracked everything because he dealt with drugs. As a senior manager, he spent a lot of time on strategic thinking, second guessing what might happen next; he was always thinking ahead. "Get in a helicopter," he used to say, "so that you could spy out the land ahead." Much of the bold and visionary approach we have taken was inspired in those early months by Tim. I am of the firm opinion that a great deal of our longevity has been down to the notion of clinical, almost pharmaceutical, drive for detail brought to our consciousness by Tim Saunders in the early days.

Tim left the UK to work in Australia for one of the world's biggest pharmaceutical companies. When he left we had a sense of loss. Our little community in St. Paul's Centre was still finding its new place in the world, and I had come to rely on Tim for strategic balance. He handed the baton over to Chris Demetriou who could not have been more different.

I remember Chris relaying the story of a work incident where, arriving late for a meeting, he sensed the urgency in the steps of the secretary, who marched him to a well-apportioned boardroom. He apologised for his late arrival and tried to settle his nerves as he placed his paperwork on the table and prepared for his pitch. They wanted a professional TV commercial producing; he wanted the business. The chairman of the board looked at Chris and asked him to begin. Pausing for effect, Chris said: "Before I begin, can I just say what a great reputation you have. My mum has had a Bendix washer-dryer for years, and it has never let her down." Before he had finished, the smirk on the assembled board members' lips indicated to Chris that something was amiss. Restraining his already growing smile, the chairman of the board leaned slightly into Chris and said, "We are really pleased that your mum's machine is working well, but we are the Bendix company that makes hydraulics for landing gear in the aviation industry." It was a common mistake to make. Amazingly, I seem to remember Chris got the job!

This was Chris in a nutshell. For a while he was a partner in a film and media company, and brought the charity a sense of enthusiasm for presenting ourselves in the best light. In meetings, he asked all the right questions and never failed to bring us back to prayer. He carried too much and over-promised, but it was all forgivable because his heart was where it needed to be. In fairness to Chris, he stepped in when Tim left and gave us more than he had spare in his busy life, and I believe we all benefited from his sacrificial service. Soon after he became Chair, his job changed bringing more pressure and time constraints.

Reflecting on the time Chris was Chair, we learned to think about our look and feel. He taught us to spend time taking a view from the customers' perspective. He was pragmatic and moved on to the next thing quickly. Chris loved to talk but it was always in search of knowledge about others – he took a real interest in you as a person. It was he who stumbled on me ejecting a driver from our building one day. The driver in question had spoken in a derogatory manner about a vulnerable adult, and I was angry. I remember he saw the funny side of it and quickly went to great lengths to move us onto something else. Chris chaired whilst we were sending aid to Kosovan refugees and building mezzanine floors; these were big and busy times.

Being a Trustee is a voluntary role, and the position of Chair carries extra responsibilities. Chris' job change meant that his days became extraordinary long, so like Tim before him the workload took him away from the charity.

Bang! A bag hit the counter with that unmistakable sound that only money can make. This was a sound I learned to respond to like a starting pistol. This sound rallied me to burst into life and seek the source of the sound. Peering around the corner into our reception, I spotted a smiling round-faced gentleman in a clerical collar. In that moment, something in my spirit resonated with his. There was nothing contrived or stiff, just a comfortable introduction.

"Well now, I'm Peterrrr Geddeeees, from Crewe Green church, and that's a collection for you." I asked if he wanted a receipt, to which he replied, "You look honest enough to me," and laughed. Accents travel poorly in print, but he had a wonderful Irish lilt. Here was my Anglican vicar, neither sought nor sent for, like the mysterious appearance of a leprechaun, Peter appeared in our reception.

In those days, several of us had been encouraging local minsters to pray together. The first prayer meeting took place at West Street Baptist Church. This seemed to grow when it moved to St. Paul's Centre which denominationally was neutral ground. Peter became one of more than ten regulars for a while. Somewhere between the donation made in our reception and that prayer meeting, Peter joined the board and was willing to take office when Chris moved away. More of Peter later… we now had an Anglican vicar.

During some meetings, talk of my lack of formal education came up and we discussed me taking an MBA. I had no interest in that direction and so visited a friend who was a lecturer at a local theological college. I embarked on a Masters in Applied Theology, as my Bible College training and experience was sufficient for entry. Malcolm Dyer, one of the lecturers, taught ethics and through our encounter I found him interested in our work. In a short time, he joined the board. However, this did not curry favour when it came to him marking my papers!

The charity was in a relaxed position in terms of growth during Malcolm's time with us. Our finance was stable, as was our operation. We had the space and resources to pause and reflect on who we, as a charity, were, and what our place in the world was. A great danger in bringing a Bible College lecturer to the Chair was the potential for theological posturing. Theologians bring with them thoughts about God – Theos meaning God, and Logis meaning knowledge. We faced the danger of that awful precipice, down which we could have engaged in circular discussions about theoretical ideas and achieved nothing. Yet, Malcolm was a pastor at heart and very much a practical people person. His compassion seemed to know no bounds, and his logical and analytical mind explored why, where, when and how. However, we had nothing to fear from his influence and everything to gain. Malcolm came with no intention of becoming the Chair and was content being on the board of Trustees.

After a few years, Peter Geddes accepted a new church appointment in Partington, near Manchester, and felt it was time for him to step down from being a Trustee and Chair. Malcolm took the seat. Through all these changes the charity grew and the team developed. I plodded on, leading and pushing the rock that is St. Paul's Centre further forward. These were not all easy times, but they were fruitful in many ways. I became aware of the challenge in leading the board as well as the team.

With each new Chair came a fresh set of challenges. For them, there was a desire for significance; it was never about power, but always about purpose of role. Malcolm and I met regularly to talk about the charity and our various operational challenges. Looking back, I recognise that this was a significant time for Malcolm as he was exploring a new direction in life. St. Paul's Centre offered him hands-on experience of the complexities of managing people and their expectations. Living locally, he could visit the centre with frequency and gained an insight and familiarity with the team. Malcolm's perceptive and enquiring nature enabled him to recognise and articulate biblical themes which correlated with our work. I recall he once spoke of the challenge he brought to his students in his tutor group. Through his encounters with St. Paul's Centre, and the many daily beneficiaries, he could see the need for Bible College students to go out and bring change to society. Malcolm became energised about the need to engage with the community.

The result of Malcolm's search led to a post as minister of a church in Formby, near Liverpool. Consequently, we lost another Chair through work transfer.

Change then came at speed and there were no offers from others on the board. In fairness, this is how charities work, and often the post of Chair is not a role most Trustees aspire to. Malcolm was my fifth chair person in eight years. Such fluency brought a sense of instability. I felt as though I carried everything, and bore the weight of the world on my shoulders. I had become the common thread holding the garment that is St. Paul's Centre together.

Sat in Malcolm's office we both prayed. These were ordinary prayers asking for help and guidance. His office was at Regents Theological College, in Nantwich, and I remember thinking we are surrounded by people searching and testing the waters for a calling to ministry. "There must be someone around this college ready to pick up the baton," I pondered.

With no obvious candidate for Chair coming to the fore, I rang Peter Geddes. My suggestion was that he return to the position for a year or so until we found a replacement. Peter knew us and the way we worked. This was in 2006 and the year or so took us to Christmas 2016!

Peter and I met every six weeks or so for a decade. We ate and talked and prayed. When a challenge came along, Peter supported me and remained professional through it all. During his time as Chair we experienced highs and lows. Times of unexpected growth were often followed by painful redundancies. Peter regularly listened to me rant, but allowed me to continue until I had got it all out. With a kind, soft Irish accent, he would say, "I can hear some sense in between the waffle." It never offended me to hear the truth from Peter and I never feared him dealing with my failings. We had true companionship in which our shared experience formed a balance to our often-challenging work.

A mark of Peter's role as Chair was in the way he never sought to be more than a board member. He had no ambition to be in the public eye, or on any publicity photos. We put him on the annual report once and he hated the whole process of posing. In the early days, Peter, Steve Coleman and I attended an awards ceremony at Bentley Motors. It was deadly boring until the photo posing. We had to stand in front of a priceless car. In 1907 Claude Johnson, Commercial and Managing Director of Rolls-Royce, ordered a car to be used as a demonstrator by the company. It was painted in aluminium paint with silver-plating, and it was called the Ghost because of its appearance. The three of us came alive and Peter became boyish. Later, I discovered his collection of model cars – all Morris Minors. Now a retired vicar, he has a green Morris Minor that he drives around in.

You have now met each of the official Chairs of the Trustee board. Now let me introduce you to another board that brought wisdom and direction, influence and fun to the work at St. Paul's Centre…

## THE SECRET CHAIRMEN

Across many years, I have sat with a lecturer, marketer and a mathematician in the corner of a small café on the edge of town; it was usually like a scene from a movie, with four men plotting who knows what. Radical in thought, with grand ideas of challenging the status quo, we met weekly. The link that held this group together, and the common thread binding us, was St. Paul's Centre. Each of us came from different corners of the community, but we were all driven by a mutual desire to see society more sustainable. We talked of politics and people.

By far the longest continuous user of St. Paul's Centre across the charity's history was Peter Foster, clocking up an impressive 28 years in the building. He was a tenant who sat through every interesting incident without making a negative comment. He has more stories to tell than anyone, but he won't. A mathematician by academic training, he became one of the first employees of Sustrans (a charitable organisation focused on sustainable transport that enables people to choose healthier, cleaner and cheaper journeys), taking a lead in developing a grass roots charity into a national force that turned over millions of pounds.

Each evening for almost two decades, Peter and I would leave St. Paul's Centre and walk our bikes to the post office in the town centre. It was our chance to debrief. The main post office closed around 2011, but we continued to walk to it before mounting our bikes to ride home. Old habits die hard.

When Sustrans moved on, Peter stayed and has been running a cycle reuse workshop in St. Paul's Centre for three years. He has mentored and inspired three young men who have gone on to find meaningful work and a new sense of direction. Peter is one of the kindest human beings I have ever encountered. His contribution in our grumpy old men's club has been invaluable in the process of keeping St. Paul's Centre on track and reflective.

"Watcha" is the word Ben first used when we met. Since his days as a dispatch cycle rider in London, he has been passionate about community cycling and is often found at meetings and in the letters page of the local newspaper discussing the subject. His lifetime in education was broken briefly whilst he worked at St. Paul's Centre helping to set up our cycle reuse project. Ben brought to our table of discussion an eccentricity which lifts the mood and challenges our conventions. Boundless energy and constant engagement have made him one of the most widely-known cycle campaigners in the county. It is hard to recall spending a time with Ben when he didn't have ten ideas to offer to any challenge we discussed. None of his ideas included can't, shouldn't or won't.

Forty years on the road, selling ideas and the benefits of marketing, Paul landed at St. Paul's Centre in retirement and volunteered his time. With so many miles on the road with his car acting as an office, Paul would be happy never to see the inside of a motor vehicle again. His gifts to us in recent years include volunteering in the cycle reuse workshop, praying every Thursday afternoon with me, and challenging the grumpy group to not demonise commercialism. Near the top of his many eyebrow-raising comments was, "At the weekend I was chatting with a group of retired generals discussing youth unemployment." Ben, Peter and I pressed for details, but none came. Paul understood that having a great idea or product finds no meaning unless someone wants it.

Meetings with these three guys on a regular basis was like having a second tier of management. In our attempts to work through the world's ills came pearls of wisdom for the charity. These chaps were close enough to the work to pick up the nuances, but detached enough to make only constructive comments. There were occasions when I shared an operational problem, and the group moved it around until the pregnant pause came and we moved the subject on. On such occasions, I came away with a new-found clarity.

In sharing this aspect of my experience, I seek to recognise the wealth of support around us. It is informal support in many ways, because there is no formal relationships. However, if Ben, Paul or Peter were Trustees or paid managers, our relationships would be so different and less fruitful. Politics and agendas would come in to play. In part, the rich dynamic is down to our maturity, breadth of experience, and even a sense of not needing to prove anything at this stage in our careers.

## SO WHAT?

The journey has not been easy. The ride often felt like a rollercoaster, completely out of my control. Loneliness and fear were often a constant companion, along with thoughts of giving in and running away. So why carry on? Why give your life to the pain and dysfunction of others? Faith in God, and a vision for change, are the short answers.

Day after day we hear, read and see news about people's needs - both local and far away. Marketers and fundraisers can predict the level of impact the news will have on charity income, and how it will change lives. An appeal with desperate circumstances has a call to action. We are given an instant way of helping: "Text DONATE to the appeal NOW!" Much of what we addressed at St. Paul's Centre over the years was not immediate, life-threating catastrophes. This is unless we include the lady who, on one Friday visiting our weekly sale, had a flat battery on her mobility scooter. Our guys delivered the scooter and woman to her home in the van for the standard delivery charge of a wardrobe. A moment of humour amid what to her was a catastrophe!

In the main, the crises we have been confronted by took some individuals decades to reach, and for some a similar timeframe to recover from. The mountains they climbed, were steep and covered with slipways back down the dangerous slopes. Over the years, we have seen the same faces re-join the path upwards having fallen earlier. No comment is made, and the word failure is always inappropriate. I do not believe I have ever met a person who is beyond change for the better. I have met many for whom the change would be slight and the cost great. Nevertheless, there is always hope, and there is always an opportunity.

In my early encounters with those on the margins of our social framework, I fantasised about having vast resources to help solve all the problems. My imagination allowed me to envisage jobs, homes and happiness for everyone. Now, more than ever before, I recognise the powerful truth contained in a sentence pinned on my door: "Men, money and material are not always the deciding factor." These words come from Malcolm Gladwell's insightful book *David and Goliath*. If nothing else, the story teaches us that big is not always best. David's incredible story encourages us to work with what we have and move with flexibility around what may appear to be unassailable giants. I keep those words on my door to remind me not to be bullied by anyone, not to be swayed by the amount of money we have (or not), and that not having in my hand the equipment does not mean we cannot do something.

The story of St. Paul's Centre is one of people with a vision for a better life. In some instances, the desired better life was their own, but mostly it was a desire for the betterment of others. The metaphor of David and Goliath is one we easily identified with in moments of great challenge. Over the history of St. Paul's Centre, there have been many challenges to overcome, each one bringing opportunities from which to adapt or to learn.

As I finish this book, it strikes me that there are many things they DID NOT tell me when they handed over the keys to the charity. Allow me to list them:

No one said how important **collaboration** with others was, people who shared our commitment to a given objective would increase the potential of success. John Ashe learned this with the LNWR in the 1860s when he invited them to join him in building St. Paul's, the church. John McCallum discovered in the 1980s this increased potential when he collaborated with Teamwork Trust. I discovered this in the 1990s when Rolls-Royce helped us articulate our plans. We have discovered the joy of working in collaboration with our local government authorities, and hundreds of others.

No one said how powerful **self-reflection** would become, that others before me had given until the tanks were empty and that few had attempted to stop them until it was too late. That self-reflection and faith would be shaped and strengthened through the crashing waves of fragile human weakness, but through it all our emotions risk not surviving. We discovered how refreshing it would be to hear a woman say, "It feels okay to not have faith here," as she stood looking at Jesus in a stained-glass window. It was refreshing because the bigger picture at St. Paul's Centre was the creation of a space in which one could reflect, doubt and lean in toward the image of Jesus.

No one said how significant **self-doubt** would be and the role it played in helping me to admit I did not know which way to turn. In September 1997, on my first day, I wrote in my diary: 'God always gives us light in the darkness whilst we desire to do his will.' That light often came in wise words given by kind friends. On the eve of crushing choices, a friend once said: "Don't do today what you can leave until tomorrow." His comment would build in me a long-term resistance to permitting people or circumstances to push me into a decision. We learned to wait and choose the most exciting opportunities. We learned that panic produces problems and a new vision is better than working with a warmed-up old one.

No one said how **flawed** our recruitment programmes would be, and that we would also find precious jewels, people that shone with beauty and grace after prayer, not just by placing advertisements. I never imagined that our journeys would be packed with excitement as we dared to be different and built a team with broken people. We encountered scores of people whose lives would converge with ours, people who joined us on the highway of life in the lane that most suited them for part of their personal journey. Each one left a mark, or a place where their presence made it all possible, more enjoyable and more valuable.

No one said how **privileged** my hands would be in linking two nations in a moment of unforgettable horror. The community of Crewe did what it could to bring relief to the suffering Kosovars in Albania. No one told me how proud I would feel eighteen years later at Christmas 2016 when, Gresa, the daughter of Kosovan refugees Genti and Adelina, visited my office with the news that she, born in Crewe, had been to Oxford for an interview to study. How honoured we are at St. Paul's Centre to have been part of their journey which began with war and destruction and is now one of settled peace and amazing prospects.

No one said how **liberating** it would be to spend two decades creatively engaged with a group of kind, thoughtful and non-judgmental people. We learned to not see those with learning difficulties as 'other.' This choice, to not identify them by inadequacies or limits, meant they were just part of the team. In all my working life, no group of people were so open and accepting, forgiving and honest. In spending our days with this group of people we were set free to be whoever we are, unhindered by imposed expectations. Geoff, Raymond and countless others living within the system of care saw themselves as having equal significance to all the others. Their gift to us was the challenge to accept the true impact of believing in human dignity, and in this we were liberated from much.

No one said how **balanced** we would become with the influence of the feminine voice. When I arrived at St. Paul's Centre in the mid-90s, the strongest voices, and therefore the ethos and atmosphere, were fuelled by male thinking. There was an absence of, and therefore a need for, the female perspective. The furniture project lent itself to hardy men and testosterone. Oily vans and heavy lifting, combined with probation lads serving community orders, blended to create discomfort for women around the place. As more women became integral to the ethos, the atmosphere changed and we all softened - not weakened, but softened. We became aware of an alternative that did not require women to think they were in a man's world. We found balance not so much in equality of gender representation, but in gender respect.

No one said how **tense** it would be balancing the different characters. That the right combination of people who pull, along with the people who push, can be like having a rocket with a brake. In growing the charity, we were blessed to have a team member who pulled us back to our core purpose. One who reminded us of why we needed to be cautious and clear, and another who brought risk and reach. I discovered forward movement was about controlling the pull and push, so that every now and then the push has more weight whilst retaining enough energy in the one pulling back to slow down when needed.

No one said how **stabilising** long-term individuals would be. Our gift has been the challenge of the transient populace of St. Paul's Centre, held in contrast against the old timers. The influence of new ideas and a fresh view is only half the ingredients required for longevity. We have been held together by the strong sense of enduring support. It has been defining and challenging to have a long-term Chair of 15 years, and business coach of 19 years. We have volunteers of 20 years-plus who possess strategic skills. Historic knowledge and personal experience of the charity have been invaluable.

If it were not for John Ashe and his belief in the need for a place of worship, there would not be a St. Paul's Centre. I'm sure he would say that it's not about a church building. If it were not for John McCallum and his drive for a home for the charity, there would not have been a St. Paul's Centre. I'm sure that he would say that it's not about the charity. In some small way, if I had been inspired to develop our furniture collection and distribution work, the charity as we know it may not have continued.

I can, however, say with complete confidence, that it is NOT about the furniture!


## ACKNOWLEDGEMENTS


First, I would like to express my gratitude to Heather Jones for her help in getting the book started, and to Stephanie Dougherty who refused to let me give in. To Macy Halford, who gave invaluable advice and practical support. June Waine, Caroline Bennett and Cheryl, my wife, offered honest encouragement, proof reading and gentle corrections to my recollections. The enclosed thoughts and accounts would never have found their way to the printed page without them.

In many ways, the book is about ordinary people doing extraordinary things in a small northern town. So, I want in this brief list to mention Jules Hornbrook, Tony Marks and Mark Potts - a trinity of local publishing champions. Thanks to them for taking what I poured from my heart and setting it in print.

Thank you must go to the people who made and continue to make St. Paul's Centre a fantastic place to be. Let me also express gratitude to countless friends, supporters and colleagues whose lives and the charity are inextricably aligned. If I have failed to mention anyone's name, my prayer is that it will appear in what the Bible calls the *Lambs Book of Life* - a better list than mine.

So, in no particular order: John & Denise McCallum, Eamon & Christine Bundred, Graham & Kerry Christopher, Josh Guildford, Joan Edwards, Tim Saunders, Peter Foster, Lynne Allan, Josh Brough, Peter Geddes, John Bennett, Roy Bradley and George Walker, Joe Watson, Simon Davies, Angelo Ikin, Averil George, Jonathon Tucker, Scott Preece, Jane Colley, Jean Dixon, Caroline Wrench, Mary Hamman, Jess Shakespeare, Pete Midgely, Gavin Evans, Isaac Newall, Sam Green, Michael Cornes, Rob James, Barbara Sheeky, Josh Saint, Ryan Brooks, Janet Taylor, Tracey Humphries, Rita Sherratt, Ben Wye, Carly Walford, Karen Ellis-Patterson, Anne Ward, Chris Leftley, Keith Boughey, Laura Doxey, Paul Chidlow, Malcolm Dyer, Sharon Roberts, Wayne Fisher, Stephen Carson, Catherine Smith, John Swainson, Jane Robinson, Joe Landy, Mark Clarke, Phil Taylor, Michael Szekely, Chris Loftus, Pam Hanscombe, June Waine, Steven Durrant, Nigel Bahrani, Audrey Wilkin, Andrew Bell, Henry Cheung, John Wilson, Robert Barker, Bob Potts, Jerry Bradley, Kenny Hewitt, Malcolm Twiss, Eva Dean, Myke Higgs, Shelley Mottram, John Mobley, Ali Thornton-Stark, Nan Watson, Kate Whyman, Andy Ollier, Anna Cheung, Vivienne Banks, Stuart Kay, Lexi Stockton, Julie Duncan, Jeff Smith, Joy Ludford, Fay Briscoe, Geoff Moran, Paul Wade, Bill Ould, Alex Morton, Paul Healey, Lorraine Owen, Rob Allen, Michael Guilfoyle, Robbie Lightfoot, Dave Curry, Raymond Shenton, Steve Coleman, Ruth Furr, Chris Coleman, Sean Savage, Paula Parry, David Darlington, Jenny Varty, Kevin Ruddy, Vera Chamberlain, Julie Austin, Derek Wright, Brian Ashpool, Emma Woolrich, Ken Patterson, Carmen Clarke, Elliott Richardson, Joy Keagan, Tracy Vyse, Colin Buckingham, Dave Nickells, Mike Larvin, David Leach, Nigel Hodder, Jon Satchwell, Esmond Simcock, Richard Holmes, Dave

Downey, Richard Froud, Graham Prawl, Kath McGlincy, Chris Demitriou, Ged Edwards, Graham Green, and Josh Leftley.

*David and Goliath*, Malcolm Gladwell (2013).
*In the name of Jesus: Reflections on Christian Leadership*, Henri J.M. Nouwen (1989).
*Memories of the Great & the Good*, Alistair Cooke (1999)